INTUITIVE EATING

A BEGINNER'S GUIDE TO THE MOST INCREDIBLE JOYUS ANTI-DIET PROGRAMME

BY:

KIRSTIN ENGELMANN

Table of Contents

INTRODUCTION

Imagine the following scenario:

You are at the office, and a co-worker brings in an assortment of cookies and baked goods for all to enjoy. It's 3 p.m., you've been working hard all day, and you eye a beautiful chocolate chip cookie. Almost immediately, your inner food critic dialogue kicks in thinking, "But cookies are full of sugar and fat," "It's not my cheat day," "If I eat this cookie, I'm going to gain weight,"and worst of all, "If I eat this cookie that means I'm being bad."

You resist eating the cookie, walk back to your office, still thinking about the cookie, but are determined not to give in to the craving. It's now 3:15 p.m., you find yourself searching your office drawers for your stash of low-calorie rice cakes, munch on a few, then munch on more. By the time 3:18 p.m. rolls around, the package is gone. You sneak around the corner to your office mates' candy jar and grab a few pieces while making friendly conversation. By the time 3:23 p.m. rolls around, you find yourself back in the office kitchen, reaching for the chocolate chip cookie, and by the time 3:25 p.m. strikes, the cookie is gone and an insurmountable wave of guilt and shame rolls in because you caved and let yourself eat the chocolate chip cookie.

Now, imagine a different scenario. You see the delicious assortment of baked goods in the staff kitchen, the chocolate chip cookie seems truly satisfying, you pick one up and take it to a relaxing location that is not your office, sit down to enjoy the taste, texture, and flavors of the cookie, and once you are satisfied, you walk back to your office to finish the rest of the workday.

Which scenario do you identify with the most? If you identify with the first scenario, you are not alone. It's estimated that about half of US adults are on a diet for weight loss purposes. If the second scenario sounded more appealing to you, then exploring intuitive eating might be right for you.

Intuitive eating is an eating style that promotes a healthy attitude toward food and body image. The idea is that you should eat when you're hungry and stop when you're full. Though this should be an intuitive process, for many people it's not.

Trusting diet books and so-called experts about what, when, and how to eat can lead you away from trusting your body and its intuition.

To eat intuitively, you may need to relearn how to trust your body. To do that, you need to distinguish between physical and emotional hunger:

- **Physical hunger.**

This biological urge tells you to replenish nutrients. It builds gradually and has different signals, such as a growling stomach, fatigue, or irritability. It's satisfied when you eat any food.

- **Emotional hunger.**

This is driven by emotional need. Sadness, loneliness, and boredom are some of the feelings that can create cravings for food, often comfort foods. Eating then causes guilt and self-hatred.

Intuitive eating is based on physical hunger rather than prescriptions from diet books and experts. Eating should satisfy physical hunger without causing guilt.

CHAPTER 1

WHAT IS INTUITIVE EATING?

Intuitive eating is an approach to health and food that has nothing to do with diets, meal plans, discipline or willpower. It teaches you how to get in touch with your body cues like hunger, fullness and satisfaction while learning to trust your body around food again. Here's an overview of intuitive eating including the science behind it, the ten principles of intuitive eating, and the difference between intuitive eating and mindful eating.

WHAT INTUITIVE EATING IS

Intuitive eating is an approach that was created by two registered dietitians, Evelyn Tribole and Elyse Resch, in 1995. Intuitive eating is a non-diet approach to health and wellness that helps you tune into your body signals, break the cycle of chronic dieting and heal your relationship with food. From a nutrition professional perspective, intuitive eating is a framework that helps us keep nutrition interventions behavior-focused instead of restrictive or rule-focused.

We are all born natural intuitive eaters. Babies cry, they eat, and then stop eating until they're hungry again. Kids innately balance out their food intake from week to week, eating when they're hungry and stopping once they feel full.

Some days they may eat a ton of food, and other days they may eat barely anything. As we grow older and rules and restrictions are set around food, we lose our inner intuitive eater. We learn to finish everything on our plate. We learn that dessert is a reward, or can be taken away if we misbehave. We are told that certain foods are good for us and others are bad – causing us to feel good about ourselves when we eat certain foods and guilty when we eat others.

Intuitive Eating is not a diet. In fact, it's exactly the opposite. There's no counting calories or macros and no making certain foods off limits. It's not about following a meal plan or measuring out your portions (in fact, that is all discouraged!). Instead, it's about re-learning to eat outside of the diet mentality, putting the focus on your internal cues (aka your intuition) like hunger, fullness and satisfaction, and moving away from external cues like food rules and restrictions.

But intuitive eating is not the 'hunger-fullness diet'. Intuitive eaters give themselves unconditional permission to eat whatever they want without feeling guilty. They rely on their internal hunger and satiety signals and trust their body to tell them when, what and how much to eat. They know when they want to at eat veggies and also when they feel like having dessert (and don't feel guilty or have any regrets with either choice).

HISTORY OF INTUITIVE EATING

The term intuitive eating was coined in 1995 as the title of a book by Evelyn Tribole and Elyse Resch. However, the concept has roots in earlier ideas.

Early pioneers include Susie Orbach, who published "Fat is a Feminist Issue" in 1978, and Geneen Roth, who has written about emotional eating since 1982.

Before that, Thelma Wayler founded a weight management program in 1973 called Green Mountain at Fox Run, based in Vermont.

The program was built on the principle that diets don't work and that lifestyle changes and personal care are more important for long-term health.

Some of the concepts of intuitive eating have been around at least since the early 1970s, though the term wasn't coined until 1995.

CHAPTER 2

PRINCIPLES OF INTUITIVE EATING

Intuitive eating is an evidence-based, mind-body health approach that was created by two registered dietitians, Evelyn Tribole and Elyse Resch, in 1995. Intuitive eating is comprised of 10 principles, which serve to either cultivate or remove obstacles to interoceptive awareness, or one's own ability to be in tune with body cues. Intuitive eating is very much a personal process, and no two individuals will experience intuitive eating the same. The underlying rationale behind it is eating when you are hungry, stopping when you are full, eating foods that truly satisfy, having unconditional permission to eat, and managing emotions without using food. Doing so allows your body to naturally adjust to its intended weight, and when you eat foods that are truly satisfying, you will naturally gravitate toward a varied and nutritionally balanced diet.

WHAT ARE THE BASIC PRINCIPLES?

Critics of intuitive eating warn that if we all started to eat whatever we wanted when we wanted, we would lose all form of self-control and nutrition principles would fly out the window. What critics tend to miss is that intuitive eating is much more nuanced than eating what you want whenever you want it, which is why there are 10 guiding principles to intuitive eating to help us along the way.

Principle 1: Rejecting the Diet Mentality

This principle gets to the heart of the matter and addresses the dangers of dieting. Right from the start, you are asked to get rid of any diet tools you are holding on to, and to let go of the pursuit of weight loss. In order to fully embrace intuitive eating, decisions about what foods to eat, when, and how much must be dictated by internal cues rather than external cues. If weight loss is the ultimate goal, food choices will be driven by external cues.

Principle 2: Honor Your Hunger

This is the first step toward re-establishing interoceptive awareness. Here, you are told to eat when you are hungry, which may be different from what you've learned when dieting, especially if you were told you needed to 'earn' the right to eat (which meant only eating when you were completely famished and ravenous with hunger). With practice, intuitive eaters become very skilled at being able to distinguish between polite hunger, taste hunger, emotional hunger, and there's even something known as practical hunger. Honoring hunger is introduced early in the process, as it's an essential piece to reconnecting the mind with body cues.

Principle 3: Making Peace with Food

This helps you begin to make peace with food—all foods. In this intuitive eating principle, you will be asking yourself a lot of questions about how and why you label foods as either "good" or "bad." In a systematic way, you will slowly navigate your way through debunking myths behind why certain foods have become off limits, why you believe you cannot trust yourself around these foods, and eventually you will be asked to incorporate these foods back into your eating routine. Some people find they benefit from additional support during this step, and seeking guidance from an experienced professional can be a great way to safely practice this step.

Principle 4: Challenge the Food Police

This principle often gets folks riled up because it's all about pushing back and challenging your own thoughts. During this principle, you will most likely be stirring up old memories from early childhood that perhaps you haven't thought about for decades. Food rules are often passed down by well-meaning family members, and in order to take inventory of the food rules that no longer serve you, it's necessary to do some deeper work here. You will also learn about the different types of "food voices" you might be challenged with, like the nutrition informant who reminds you of calorie counts and grams of added sugar. You will also learn how to turn unhelpful internal dialogue into helpful, nurturing messages.

Principle 5: Respect Your Fullness

This one does not immediately follow principle 2 as you might expect. That is because it is much easier to recognize when you are hungry and to eat when hungry, and a bit more challenging to recognize the different levels of fullness and actually stop eating when you've reached that comfortably full level. Here, again, we find well-intentioned family food rules coming into play—if you grew up with the expectation that you must eat every single last speck of food off your plate before you were allowed to leave the table or have dessert, this principle may take time to undo that hardwired habit.

Principle 6: Discover the Satisfaction Factor

This is probably one of the most fundamental principles of the entire concept of intuitive eating. When we choose food based on flavor, taste, texture, aroma, and not based on fat grams or calories, the eating experience is more satisfying, and we are actually likely to eat less food in the long run. During this principle, you will be asked to consider motivations behind food selection, and you will be asked to go on a sensory journey with your food choices, reconnecting with all of the different complexities of foods that are truly satisfying to you. You might also find yourself being pleasantly surprised to find that previously off-limit foods are actually not that satisfying at all!

Principle 7: Honor Your Feelings Without Using Food

This requires you to expand your current toolbox of emotional coping mechanisms. For many adults, when faced with an emotionally stimulating situation, food is used as a solution to self-soothe. This makes perfect sense for those who were raised in families where food was used as a reward or as a comforting proxy for upset feelings. In this principle, you will learn how to better identify and label your emotions, learn how to sit with uncomfortable emotions, and learn how to manage emotions in productive ways rather than silencing them with food. It is often at this point in the process that some people recognize they would benefit from additional support to help address past traumas.

Principle 8: Respect Your Body

This principle of intuitive eating is all about getting into the habit of addressing your body with kindness and respect, and recognizing that it has continued to show up for you, despite years of body abuse from dieting. The authors and creators of intuitive eating are very intentional about emphasizing the fact that in order to take care of something, you must respect it first. Respecting your body does not require you to fully accept it the way it is, but it does help you see all the wonder your body does.

Principle 9: Exercise—Feel the Difference

This helps readers debunk exercise-related myths and broadens the idea of exercise into general movement. When we move our bodies for enjoyment rather than for weight loss purposes, we are much more motivated to move more often during the day. Many chronic dieters have an adverse reaction to the term "exercise," so this principle requires a gentle reframing of what movement can look like. You will rediscover the types of movement that bring your body joy, that lifts your mood, and makes you actually look forward to that activity.

Principle 10: Honor Your Health—Gentle Nutrition

This principle is saved until the very end so that the intuitive eating concept doesn't fall under the diet category. In this principle, concepts of nutrition science are discussed;

however, one does not need to get caught up in the nutrition minutiae, because the evidence shows that when you are eating intuitively, you will naturally gravitate toward a more nutritionally balanced way of eating. Yes, nutrition really can be that simple!

What Are The Health Benefits Of Intuitive Eating?

To date, there have been over 90 studies investigating the benefits of intuitive eating. Individuals who score higher on the Intuitive Eating Scale benefit physically, psychologically, and emotionally.

To summarize, intuitive eaters, across all age groups, genders, and ethnicities have the following in common:

- Lower body mass index (BMI)
- Lower triglycerides
- Higher HDL (the "good" cholesterol)
- Higher self-esteem, well-being, optimism, body appreciation and acceptance, proactive coping skills, psychological hardiness, unconditional self-regard, pleasure from eating, and eating a variety of foods
- Less internalized ideal of being thin, eating disorders, emotional eating, and self-silencing

Critics of intuitive eating warn that if you eat whatever you want, whenever you want, you will lose all sense of control and will not feel motivated to eat a nutritionally adequate or balanced diet. However, quite the opposite is true! A 2006 study found that intuitive eaters ate a more diverse diet without turning to junk food, took more pleasure in their eating, and ate a healthier diet than those who did not eat intuitively.

Intuitive Eating has been proven beneficial and effective globally in children, adolescents, adults, and in people with different chronic diseases such as diabetes. The key point to keep in mind is that intuitive eating is very much a personal process. As an example, someone in the early stages of recovery from an eating disorder may not be ready to rely on hunger or fullness cues, but they can start working on other principles such as challenging the food police and respecting their bodies.

How Can Someone Get Started With Intuitive Eating?

Fortunately, there are loads of great resources for those who are interested in getting started with intuitive eating! You can get yourself a copy of the Intuitive Eating book and accompanying workbook. There are online support groups and in-person support groups popping up all over the world. You can also find a certified intuitive eating counselor in your area, and some even provide virtual coaching.

Is This An Effective Way To Lose Weight?

The authors of intuitive eating make it very clear from the beginning that intuitive eating is NOT a weight loss program, and that in order to fully embrace intuitive eating, weight loss goals must be put on the back burner or else food choices will be made with the motivation for weight loss and not with the motivation for satisfaction. A 2012 study shows that individuals who score higher on the Intuitive Eating Scale tend to have lower BMIs. This suggests that people who eat in response to hunger and satiety cues have unconditional permission to eat and cope with emotions without using food, and they are less likely to engage in eating behaviors that lead to weight gain. However, most individuals who embark on the intuitive eating journey quickly realize that the benefits gained go so far beyond weight loss, that weight loss soon becomes a non-issue

CHAPTER 3

BENEFITS OF INTUITIVE EATING

Unlike dieting, learning how to eat intuitively is not measured by pounds lost or inches shed (in fact, weighing yourself can hinder the intuitive eating process – more on that here). When you first start your intuitive eating journey, it can feel like a slow and scary process.

But over time, you'll start noticing a lot of changes happening in varying areas of your life. Although food freedom and a better relationship with food are one of the benefits of intuitive eating, you will also see tremendous benefits in your physical, mental, emotional health, and spiritual health.

There are over 100 research studies looking at intuitive eating and intuitive eating has been shown to have many health outcomes, including:

- Improved cholesterol levels
- Better body image
- Higher self-esteem
- Improved metabolism
- Decreased rates of disordered and emotional eating
- Diminished stress levels

- Increased satisfaction with life

These mental and physical health benefits are fantastic and it's so exciting to see intuitive eating be studied so frequently. But when you're in the midst of the intuitive eating process, and are working to come to terms with your relationship to food and your body, it can be hard to relate to these science-y benefits.

So I decided to put together a different kind of list of intuitive eating benefits – one that you may be able to relate to more easily.

BENEFITS OF INTUITIVE EATING

You can detect – and honor – hunger cues. You are able to notice when your body feels hunger, and honor that hunger by feeding it. Even if it's late at night, or it's "only" been X hours since your last meal, or if you think you already ate enough today – you trust your body when it tells you it's hungry.

You know what foods you like and dislike. Now that you're not eating based on external signals, you are able to explore food and figure out what you like and don't like. Often times, you'll find that some of the "forbidden" foods you might have binged on in the past, you realize you don't even like. Alternatively, you have the freedom to explore foods without the "good" and "bad" chains, which often means you'll find a whole bunch of foods or recipes that you never knew you could love.

You have less guilty thoughts surrounding food. You are able to shut down your inner food police and can enjoy a variety of foods without feelings of judgment or guilt.

Food no longer is a moral issue. Labels like "good" and "bad" fade away. You don't categorize food anymore and are able to remove yourself from the guilt you once associated with certain foods. You no longer feel like you've been "good" or "bad" related to your food choices and you know that you are worthy no matter what you eat.

Food tastes better. When you get rid of the guilt and anxiety surrounding food, there is more room for taste. You are able to be more present and pay attention to the taste, the texture, and smell, which leads to more enjoyment.

You are able to notice how certain foods make you feel. You have developed a much better relationship with food and can detect your fullness and satiety cues. You know which foods make you feel good and energized and you know which foods don't.

You have more energy. As you become more in tune with your body you're able to recognize what foods make you feel your best. You find that you have more energy consistently throughout the day and you figure out which foods help your energy levels and which ones don't.

You don't get cravings as often. When you start to re-establish trust with your body and honor your hunger and fullness cues, your cravings will become less frequent.

Your self-confidence increases. You've stripped away the guilt you once attached to eating certain foods and have learned to trust your body. You know that what you eat does not define you. Your overall self-confidence increases as you learn to trust yourself and live an unapologetic life. You don't feel like you owe anyone else your health or your body.

Your relationships with friends and family improve. When you no longer have so much stress and anxiety surrounding food, you free up space to just be and enjoy the food – and the people – around you. You can engage in social interactions more often and can put your attention on spending time with friends and family, rather than worrying about your diet.

You are more flexible. Your thinking is no longer "all or nothing" and you have more brain space to be flexible, and changes – like spontaneous dinner plans or a restaurant that is closed – don't throw off your entire day.

You develop a better relationship with exercise and actually enjoy it. You see exercise as a form of self-care and no longer as a means to burn off a certain number of calories. You embrace intuitive movement and only do the exercise you enjoy. You don't feel guilty when you take a rest day.

You are able to keep "trigger" foods around your house. You buy food you love at the grocery store and store it once you get home and don't give it any more thought. You eat it when you feel like it and sometimes you might even forget it's there.

You can leave leftovers on your plate. You can detect when you are full and do not feel obliged to always finish everything on your plate.

You approach things with curiosity instead of judgment. Using curiosity allows you to take a step back and gain perspective. You can be thoughtful and reflective and find the grey area, instead of utilizing black and white thinking. You can learn from your actions, instead of beating yourself up for them.

You have more time on your hands. Now that you're not preoccupied with thoughts of food, you have more headspace and time to do other things. You can explore other hobbies and ways of filling your time.

You try things you've never tried before. This could be different foods, different cuisines or different activities. Your increase in self-confidence allows you to open up your world and do things you wouldn't have done before. For example, you are able to go out to dinner without having to scan the menu beforehand or you are able to throw on a swimsuit and not think twice about what others may think.

You are nicer to yourself. You learn self-compassion skills and begin to treat yourself as you would a friend or loved one. You are kind and understanding to yourself, and instead of beating yourself up, you think about ways you can comfort and care for yourself.

You find other coping mechanisms. You develop several tools to help manage stress and emotions. Food may be one of them, but it's not the only coping tool in your arsenal. You are also able to emotionally eat, recognize why it is happening, and do it in a way that feels helpful and supportive.

Your overall mood improves. You don't feel guilty eating foods you were once fearful of and you don't let food affect your mood anymore. You know how to properly fuel your body and are able to discern what makes you feel good physically and mentally.

Your digestion improves. When you eat in a stressed state, your digestion can completely shut down. This can cause constipation and lead to a host of gastrointestinal related issues. But as your food anxiety and stress decreases, and you get to learn how certain foods affect your body, you may experience less gastrointestinal symptoms.

You eat more mindfully. You tune into your body's hunger, satiety, and fullness cues and are able to take the time to decipher when you reach each state. You take your time eating and savor each bite.

You are more satisfied with life. You feel happier overall and are able to seek pleasure from things other than food. You are not constantly worried about what other people are thinking of you and can live your life unapologetically in a way that supports your wants and needs.

You develop a new sense of awareness. You are more mindful, not just when you eat, but in general, you are more present throughout the day. This can mean increased body awareness, better connection and conversations with others, and more

CHAPTER 4

THE SCIENCE BEHIND INTUITIVE EATING

Until recently, evidence that intuitive eating promoted weight loss was largely testimonial, but a group of studies published in the last few years has lent more credence to the claims.

Especially influential is research from Tylka. Before investigating intuitive eating, Tylka specialized in people with eating disorders, focusing on those who fell along the spectrum of disordered eating without being symptomatic enough to actually be diagnosed. Some 40 percent of Americans qualified for this broader category, she found.

As a group, these people were often unhappy, obsessed with their weight and suffering from body-image problems, whether they were overweight or not.

Those who didn't fall on the spectrum, she discovered, seemed to be intuitive eaters whose habits resembled those of the people Tribole and Resch had described in their book.

By 2006, Tylka had laid the scientific basis for researching the eating style. She created a scale that defined and then measured the traits of intuitive eaters: Those who qualified could be defined by 21 traits in three broad categories, including unconditional permission to eat, eating from physical rather than emotional cues, and relying on internal hunger and satiety cues.

Tylka used her scale to study more than 1,400 people, determining that intuitive eaters have a higher sense of well-being and lower body weight and do not seem to internalize the "thin ideal." Later research on 1,260 college women found intuitive eaters shared a series of empowering traits: They were optimistic and resilient, skilled at social problem solving, and had good self-esteem.

A study Tylka published in 2010 showed that parental pressure to restrict eating in childhood translated to higher BMI in adults. The pressure backfired by disconnecting individuals from their natural hunger and satiety cues, she posits. Indeed, her adult participants reported "a lower tendency to eat when physically hungry and stop eating when full."

While the studies can't really prove causality — no one can say whether eating styles are determined by life circumstances and personality traits, or vice versa — Tylka sees the relationship as "bidirectional." She sums up her findings this way: "Attending to physiological signals of hunger and satiety are uniquely connected to well-being, and to lower body mass."

How Hormones Drive Our Food Cravings

No matter where experts stand on intuitive eating, they universally agree that restrictive diets have failed, en masse. Most of the diets we tap today are still rooted in the old "calories in, calories out" model — a straightforward equation in which every morsel of food and every iota of exercise is evaluated on the basis of its caloric value. This mechanistic formula implies that the overweight among us must simply be too lazy, ignorant or lacking in self-control to regulate themselves accordingly, and are thus entirely responsible for their own plight.

But important new research has proven this line of thinking quite wrong, and that's one reason intuitive eating is getting a second look from experts who might previously have written it off.

What the new research shows, according to George Blackburn, MD, PhD, director of the Center for the Study of Nutrition Medicine at Harvard Medical School, is that the stomach and other metabolically critical parts of the body don't just process foodborne calories. Rather, they are responsible for sending dozens of chemical and hormonal messages to the brain, where what we think of as hunger reallyresides.

One key hormone in this system is ghrelin, the only biomolecule found to stimulate the hunger center in the hypothalamus of the brain. Ghrelin is released from the stomach in response not only to physiological hunger — triggered when cells are short on energy — but also to pleasure seeking and stress.

Experiments have shown that people injected with ghrelin eat 30 percent more — perhaps because the hormone gravitates to the same brain area responsible for addictive behaviors. Conventional diets based on calorie restriction limit energy to cells, boosting ghrelin and driving hunger that may be almost impossible to resist as time goes on.

Ever wonder why you overeat when stressed out? The stress hormone, cortisol, triggers the body to produce extra ghrelin. That ghrelin works on the brain's pleasure centers to calm you down, but you pay the price in extra weight.

Then there's leptin, one of a series of "satiety hormones" produced by fat cells that tell the brain it's time to put your fork down. There was a time when scientists celebrated the discovery of leptin, hoping that supplements would suppress appetite and keep weight under control. But for the overweight, leptin is a dead end; levels are already elevated in the obese, but their cell receptors are resistant, much like diabetics are resistant to insulin.

The obese have plenty of leptin, in other words, but it no longer has an effective place to land. The chemistry is complex, but the takeaway message for lifelong dieters is disturbingly simple: Calorie restriction elevates ghrelin, driving the hunger that sparks overeating and weight gain. The situation worsens as the failed diets stack up and the years go by. The resulting obesity renders the brain resistant to leptin, the very hormone that is supposed to help put the brakes on our appetites.

How to Eat Intuitively

Greeting our desire for food with conscious awareness rather than white-knuckled self-control is an essential priority of intuitive eating — in part because most of us have been socially and environmentally programmed to eat without much consciousness at all.

"Food is everywhere in brightly colored packages," observes Lynn Rossy, PhD, a health psychologist who teaches mindfulness in her intuitive-eating workshops at the T. E. Atkins University of Missouri Wellness Program in Columbia. "But what is in the food, and how are we using it? Are we hungry or full when we decide to eat? Are we eating to disengage from our emotions, or to get pleasure? Are we eating when we are really hungry for something else that we would find by looking to other parts of our lives? We make so many food choices every day, but we're so busy we're not paying attention. In order for someone to become an intuitive eater, that has to change."

Intuitive eaters must tune in to not just hunger and satiety, but also mood. "Emotion can impact the digestive system and mimic the feelings of hunger," explains Rossy, "but practicing mindfulness can help you tell the difference. It gets easier over time."

Susan Albers, PsyD, author of Eating Mindfully: How to End Mindless Eating and Enjoy a Balanced Relationship with Food (New Harbinger, 2003), found that intuitive eaters can often handle cravings just by slowing down. As with other forms of impulse, simply stopping to ponder the source of a craving can help you realize that it isn't about hunger at all.

Food can be a drug, she explains, in that it stimulates the feel-good neurotransmitter, serotonin. But those mindful enough to grasp that they are eating to boost mood, not appease hunger, can seek the fix through a healthy alternative like exercise, meditation or social connection.

The key, says Albers, is awareness: "If you remove that comfort eating, you must consciously put something back to take its place, be it meditation or massage. The mindful eater recognizes and respects physiological hunger — if you are really hungry, it is important to respond."

Nutrition consultant Marc David, MA, author of The Slow Down Diet: Eating for Pleasure, Energy & Weight Loss (Healing Arts, 2005), has his clients focus on the quality of the food itself. His rationale is simple: Higher-quality food — real, fresh, flavorful and organic — is nutrient dense and inherently satisfying.

"Yes, many of us eat too much," says David, founder and director of the Boulder, Colo.–based Institute for the Psychology of Eating. "But we do so, to a degree, because our food is nutrient deficient. It lacks the vitamins, minerals, enzymes, and all the undiscovered X-factors and energies we require. The brain senses these deficiencies and wisely responds to this absence of vital chemistry by commanding us to undertake the most sensible survival strategy: Eat more food."

One key to getting such cravings under control, David asserts, may simply be to upgrade the quality of the food we eat, then notice how we experience it. "Stop and see how you feel following every meal," he suggests.

Is Intuitive Eating for Everybody?

In the end, only you can intuit which foods are right for you — and whether your cravings are driven by a nutritional need, an emotional one — or, as is often the case, both. To the extent you're capable of discerning such things, and motivated to do so, you may have success with intuitive eating as a weight-loss strategy.

Critics of intuitive eating point out, though, that for many, the approach has some very real limitations. For one thing, notes Elson Haas, MD, some people crave the very foods that are making them sick — much like an addict may crave a drug, despite the overall damage that it does. Indulging cravings for those foods could set you up for an inflammatory and immune response that worsens biochemical imbalances rather than ameliorating them. Even nutritious foods like yogurt, nuts and whole grains are not going to produce good results for those folks who have allergies or intolerances to them.

Also, cravings for sugar, dairy products and caffeine do not typically abate with indulgence, Haas notes, but instead tend to drive inflammation, water retention, brain fog — and still more craving.

The only way out of that rut, says Haas, author of The False Fat Diet: The Revolutionary 21-Day Program for Losing the Weight You Think Is Fat (Ballantine Books, 2001), is to heal and re-regulate the body's disrupted biochemistry. This necessarily involves a certain amount of self-control in the short term, he notes, but for a totally different and arguably better reason than controlling calories. The goal here is to clear your system of the biochemical factors that are confounding it — and your weight-loss efforts.

Even without an allergy or food addiction, though, intuitive eating may be hard to master for the obese, many of whom may struggle with imbalances in blood sugar and brain chemistry that have become entrenched by years of dysfunctional eating. Such imbalances can effectively compromise the body-based intuition that individuals require to put intuitive eating techniques to work.

That was part of the message when the Society for the Study of Ingestive Behavior held its annual meeting in Pittsburgh this July. University of Illinois researchers reported that a diet consistently high in fat restricted the neurotransmitter dopamine in the striatum (the part of the brain associated with reward). The upshot was that rats on high-fat fare had to eat more than their brethren on a low-fat diet for the same sense of reward.

University of Pennsylvania researchers reported that leptin — the fullness hormone — activates the hippocampus, and this process may be impaired by obesity, making it harder for obese individuals to muster self-control.

And Yale scientists scanned the brains of human subjects exposed to the smell and taste of food: The brains of normal-weight participants reacted differently, depending on their level of hunger. But obese participants' brains reacted to taste and smell no matter what the status of their hunger, driving them to eat long after getting full.

So, is intuitive eating for you? Only you can decide. If you're out to maintain your weight or drop a few pounds, intuitive eating may be an ideal strategy. If you've experienced little luck with restrictive dieting in the past, intuitive eating may help you rethink your whole approach to food. But if you are obese or dealing with disrupted biochemistry as the result of food intolerances, you may want to seek some professional nutrition counseling to rebalance your body and brain before you give intuitive eating a try.

Either way, keep in mind that intuitive eating is a package deal — the practices of conscious attention can't be separated from the "eat what you like" philosophy. You can't just cave in to cravings without being willing to question them first.

Nor can intuitive eating be practiced effectively in a vacuum devoid of sensible food practices. For example, Haas notes, "Planning ahead with a good menu enables you to have healthy foods available when you need them" — something that may be tough to pull off if you always eat on the spur of the moment.

All of us, though, could probably benefit from tuning in to our bodies more often. "The body has spectacular wisdom," says Marc David. "We just have to listen to access it."

There are now over 100 research studies that have shown the benefits of intuitive eating. The studies show that intuitive eating is associated with:

- Higher self-esteem
- Better body image
- More satisfaction with life
- Optimism and well-being
- Proactive coping skills
- Lower body mass indexes
- Higher HDL cholesterol levels
- Lower Triglyceride levels
- Lower rates of emotional eating
- Lower rates of disordered eating

How to Navigate Your Fear of Weight Gain

Recently I was talking with a new client about intuitive eating, when they said "This sounds great, but what will happen to my weight?"

If this is one of your barriers to learning more about intuitive eating or healing your relationship with food, you are not alone. Having these fears about change in weight or weight gain, when letting go of strict rules around food and your diet, is totally normal. This is one of the most common conversations that I have with clients – whether they're new to intuitive eating, or not. So today I'm digging into the fear around weight gain, sharing some tips to unpack more about where that fear comes from, and how to navigate this struggle while continuing your journey to finding more peace with food and your body.

"I'm still not sure I'd be okay with gaining weight. Can I still start working on intuitive eating even if I feel that way?"

Yes! This desire to lose weight is normal, given that we live in a very weight-centric and fatphobic culture. For most of us, it's not realistic to wake up one day and love everything about your body or expect to 'snap out of' beliefs and feelings you have about weight. BUT that said, it is possible over time

When you ask what you can expect to happen to your weight when you stop dieting, the answer is: I don't know. And you don't know.

We can't guarantee where your body will fall when no longer dieting or weight cycling. The unknown can be scary, so it's okay for that to feel uncomfortable. The idea of not being in control of your weight can be frightening, especially because the messages diet culture has been selling you for years is that you *can* and should be controlling your weight...and if you're not, then "you must not be trying hard enough or doing the right plan". (Ahem, diet culture)

This puts all the pressure on you to make it seem like being a certain weight is your moral obligation as a human, and that failing to do so is a personal failure, rather than a failure of the diet itself.

Evelyn Tribole, Registered Dietitian and co-author of Intuitive Eating put it well when she said: "The weight loss industry is the only industry where a customer buys a product that doesn't work and the manufacturer blames the customer."

Aka: It's not you, it's the diet!

Where Does The Fear Of Weight Gain Or Change In Weight Come From?

Let's start unpacking. Think about your history with diets and dieting. Have you been able to 'control' your weight? The statistics show us otherwise. in general, dieting is more effective at continuing weight cycling – that is losing then regaining weight – instead of the advertised "sustained weight loss".

If you have lost weight or felt in control through dieting, what was the cost of doing so? How was your social or family life affected? Did you feel restricted or out of control around certain foods? Did you find eating to be something that caused guilt, stress or anxiety?

While diets paint the picture of easy, long term change in weight, most people I work with have experienced the exact opposite. What diets really sell you isn't the result, it's the illusion of that control. This contributes to a complicated relationship with your weight, your body, and food in general.

The fear of weight gain first comes from the idea that each individual has the ability to control and manipulate their weight to a certain specific number or range. And further, that it's a person's responsibility to do so; and not doing or choosing not to is a personal failure. In reality: this is diet culture's failure, not yours.

The other place that this fear comes from is some likely deeply rooted fatphobia (TW: this Guardian.com article contains numbers and mention of disordered eating behaviors).

You've been brought up in a society that values thinness and treats people differently for their body size, and you may have some personal experiences or trauma that supports those beliefs as well. This isn't uncomplicated, but at the end of the day, all people and bodies are deserving of respect. This is what the Health at Every Size® movement is grounded in as well.

There are many layers to our relationship with food, body and our weight. Beginning to look into those relationships and starting to question where these beliefs stem from, and if they're the ones you want to keep, can be a big step in navigating your relationship with your body.

You might even realize that even in exploring a non-diet approach, the messages you are receiving are coming from mostly thin, white, able-bodied, young women. Diversifying your feeds and seeing people with all different bodies being confident, successful and happy helps to challenge and bring awareness to these assumptions and biases. We are all learning and unlearning!

Some questions to ask yourself:

- Where did my fear of weight gain come from?
- Why do I value thinness?
- What is my opinion on those in larger bodies?

- Why do I think I am unlovable if my pant size increases?

- How are these opinions and beliefs impacting me? Are they in-line with my values?

- What evidence do I have for or against these beliefs?

"Ok, but how can I navigate all of these things while still healing my relationship with food and my body?"

You're doing it! Reading this blog post, exploring these assumptions and where your values and beliefs have come from, and sitting with them is part of the process. If you're at the start of your journey, it may be helpful to put the desire for weight loss on a back or side burner. By not having it front-and-center as your metric for progress or success, you can focus on other ways to measure progress.

To have fear and anxiety around weight is normal and is something that you, your therapist and/or dietitian can continue navigating. Dieting and weight loss focused language keeps us constantly planning for the future, what you 'would do' or be deserving of once you lose weight.

This can hold you back from enjoying, respecting and taking care of your body in the present. When weight loss is on the back burner, you can think about what you can appreciate your body for today. How can you make yourself feel more comfortable and confident today? What's a goal or something fun you want to do short-term that doesn't require changing your body?

It can also help to ask yourself, what is underneath that desire for weight loss? For most people, the goal of being in a smaller body is really the desire be loved, respected, valued, seen as worthy, as successful, etc. Diet culture may tell you that those things are conditional on size, but they are not.

CHAPTER 5

MINDFUL EATING - A BEGINNER'S GUIDE

- Mindful eating is a technique that helps you gain control over your eating habits.

- It has been shown to promote weight loss, reduce binge eating, and help you feel better.

- This book explains what mindful eating is, how it works, and what you need to do to get started.

WHAT IS MINDFUL EATING?

- Mindful eating is based on mindfulness, a Buddhist concept.

- Mindfulness is a form of meditation that helps you recognize and cope with your emotions and physical sensations.

- It's used to treat many conditions, including eating disorders, depression, anxiety, and various food-related behaviors.

- Mindful eating is about using mindfulness to reach a state of full attention to your experiences, cravings, and physical cues when eating..

Fundamentally, mindful eating involves:

- food has on your feelings and figure
- Appreciating you Eating slowly and without distraction
- Listening to physical hunger cues and eating only until you're full
- Distinguishing between true hunger and non-hunger triggers for eating
- Engaging your senses by noticing colors, smells, sounds, textures, and flavors
- Learning to cope with guilt and anxiety about food
- Eating to maintain overall health and well-being
- Noticing the effects r food
- These things allow you to replace automatic thoughts and reactions with more conscious, healthier responses.

Mindful eating relies on mindfulness, a form of meditation. Mindful eating is about developing awareness of your experiences, physical cues, and feelings about food.

WHY SHOULD YOU TRY MINDFUL EATING?

Today's fast-paced society tempts people with an abundance of food choices.

On top of that, distractions have shifted attention away from the actual act of eating toward televisions, computers, and smartphones.

Eating has become a mindless act, often done quickly. This can be problematic, since it takes your brain up to 20 minutes to realize you're full.

If you eat too fast, the fullness signal may not arrive until you have already eaten too much. This is very common in binge eating.

By eating mindfully, you restore your attention and slow down, making eating an intentional act instead of an automatic one.

What's more, by increasing your recognition of physical hunger and fullness cues, you are able to distinguish between emotional and true, physical hunger.

You also increase your awareness of triggers that make you want to eat, even though you're not necessarily hungry.

By knowing your triggers, you can create a space between them and your response, giving you the time and freedom to choose how to react.

Mindful eating helps you distinguish between emotional and physical hunger. It also increases your awareness of food-related triggers and gives you the freedom to choose your response to them.

MINDFUL EATING AND WEIGHT LOSS

It's well known that most weight loss programs don't work in the long term.

Around 85% of people with obesity who lose weight return to or exceed their initial weight within a few years.

Binge eating, emotional eating, external eating, and eating in response to food cravings have been linked to weight gain and weight regain after successful weight loss.

Chronic exposure to stress may also play a large role in overeating and obesity.

The vast majority of studies agree that mindful eating helps you lose weight by changing your eating behaviors and reducing stress.

A 6-week group seminar on mindful eating among people with obesity resulted in an average weight loss of 9 pounds (4 kg) during the seminar and the 12-week follow-up period.

Another 6-month seminar resulted in an average weight loss of 26 pounds (12 kg) — without any weight regain in the following 3 months.

By changing the way you think about food, the negative feelings that may be associated with eating are replaced with awareness, improved self-control, and positive emotions.

When unwanted eating behaviors are addressed, your chances of long-term weight loss success are increased.

Mindful eating may aid weight loss by changing eating behaviors and reducing the stress associated with eating.

Mindful Eating And Binge Eating

Binge eating involves eating a large amount of food in a short amount of time, mindlessly and without control.

It has been linked to eating disorders and weight gain, and one study showed that almost 70% of people with binge eating disorder are obese.

Mindful eating may drastically reduce the severity and frequency of binge eating episodes.

One study found that after a 6-week group intervention in women with obesity, binge eating episodes decreased from 4 to 1.5 times per week. The severity of each episode decreased as well.

Mindful eating can help prevent binge eating. It can both reduce the frequency of binges and the severity of each binge.

MINDFUL EATING AND UNHEALTHY EATING BEHAVIORS

In addition to being an effective treatment for binge eating, mindful eating methods have also been shown to reduce:

- **Emotional eating.** This is the act of eating in response to certain emotions.
- **External eating.** This occurs when you eat in response to environmental, food-related cues, such as the sight or smell of food.

Unhealthy eating behaviors like these are the most commonly reported behavioral problems in people with obesity.

Mindful eating gives you the skills you need to deal with these impulses. It puts you in charge of your responses instead of at the whim of your instinct.

Mindful eating may effectively treat common, unhealthy eating behaviors like emotional and external eating.

How To Practice Mindful Eating

To practice mindfulness, you need a series of exercises and meditations.

Many people find it helpful to attend a seminar, online course, or workshop on mindfulness or mindful eating.

However, there are many simple ways to get started, some of which can have powerful benefits on their own:

- Eat more slowly and don't rush your meals.

- Chew thoroughly.

- Eliminate distractions by turning off the TV and putting down your phone.

- Eat in silence.

- Focus on how the food makes you feel.

- Stop eating when you're full.

- Ask yourself why you're eating, whether you're truly hungry, and whether the food you chose is healthy.

To begin with, it's a good idea to pick one meal per day to focus on these points.

Once you have the hang of it, mindfulness will become more natural. Then you can focus on implementing these habits into more meals.

Mindful eating takes practice. Try to eat more slowly, chew thoroughly, remove distractions, and stop eating when you're full.

Mindful eating is a powerful tool to regain control of your eating.

If conventional diets haven't worked for you, this technique is worth considering.

SCIENCE-BACKED TIPS TO STOP MINDLESS EATING

On average, you make more than 200 decisions about food each day — but you're only aware of a small fraction of them.

The rest are performed by your unconscious mind and can lead to mindless eating, which may cause you to overeat, promoting weight gain.

Here are 13 science-backed tips to stop mindless eating.

Share on Pinterest

1. Use visual reminders

Behavioral scientists believe one of the main reasons people overeat is because they rely on external rather than internal cues to decide whether they feel hungry or full.

Naturally, this can lead you to eat more than you need to.

To demonstrate this point, researchers provided participants with an unlimited amount of chicken wings while watching a long, televised sporting event.

Half of the tables were continuously cleaned, while the bones were left to accumulate on other tables. People with bones on their tables ate 34% less, or 2 fewer chicken wings, than people who had their tables cleaned.

Another experiment used bottomless bowls to slowly refill some participants' soups as they ate.

Those who ate from bottomless bowls consumed 73% more — amounting to roughly 113 extra calories — than those who ate from normal bowls.

Yet, those who ate more soup didn't feel fuller. Most also estimated their calorie intake to be the same as those eating from the regular soup bowls.

These two studies show that people tend to rely on visual cues, such as chicken bones or the amount of soup left, to decide whether they're full or still hungry.

To make this natural tendency work in your favor, keep evidence of what you eat in front of you. Examples include the empty beer bottles you drank at a barbecue or the plates used for previous courses at an all-you-can-eat buffet.

Use visual reminders of the foods and drinks you consume to help you stay mindful of how much you've already consumed.

2. Favor smaller packages

Another external cue that can cause you to overeat is the size of your food packaging.

Known as the portion size effect, it may contribute to significant weight gain over time.

On the other hand, packages that include pause points may help diminish this effect, as they give you time to decide whether to keep eating.

For example, participants eating potato chips from cans of Pringles in which every 7th or 14th chip was dyed red ate 43–65% fewer chips than those eating from cans with no dyed chips.

Similarly, people eating from a large bag of 200 M&Ms consumed 31 more candies — 112 extra calories — than people given 10 small baggies of 20 M&Ms.

Favoring smaller packages can help you reduce the number of calories you consume by up to 25% without even noticing.

3. Use smaller plates and taller glasses

Studies show that people tend to eat 92% of the food they serve themselves.

Therefore, reducing the amount of food you serve yourself can make a significant difference in the number of calories you consume.

One easy way to reduce portion sizes without noticing the change is to use smaller plates and taller glasses.

That's because big plates tend to make your food portions look small, encouraging you to serve yourself more food.

Simply using 9.5-inch (24-cm) plates instead of 12.5-inch (32-cm) plates can help you easily eat up to 27% less food.

Additionally, studies show that using tall, thin glasses instead of wide, short ones can reduce the amount of liquids you pour yourself by up to 57%.

Therefore, pick wide, short glasses to help you drink more water and tall, thin ones to help you limit alcohol and other high-calorie beverages.

Replacing large plates with smaller ones and wide, short glasses with tall, thin ones are two easy ways to reduce your portion sizes and limit the effects of mindless eating.

4. Decrease variety

Research shows that having a wider variety of food options can lead you to eat up to 23% more.

Experts label this phenomenon "sensory-specific satiety." The basic idea is that your senses tend to get numb after you're exposed to the same stimulus many times — for instance, the same flavors.

Having a wide variety of flavors in the same meal can delay this natural numbing, pushing you to eat more.

Simply believing there's more variety can also fool you. Researchers found that participants given bowls with 10 colors of M&Ms ate 43 more candies than those given bowls with 7 colors, despite all M&Ms tasting the same.

To make sensory-specific satiety work for you, try limiting your choices. For instance, pick only two appetizers at once during cocktail parties and stick to ordering the same drinks throughout the evening.

Keep in mind that this mainly applies to candy and junk food. Eating a variety of healthy foods, such as fruits, vegetables, and nuts, is beneficial to your health.

Reducing the variety of food flavors, colors, and textures you're exposed to will help prevent you from eating more junk food than your body needs.

5. Keep some foods out of sight

Researchers report that the popular saying, "out of sight, out of mind" applies particularly well to mindless eating.

To illustrate this point, one study gave secretaries Hershey's Kisses in covered bowls that were either clear, so they could see the candy, or solid, so they could not.

Those given clear bowls opened them to get candy 71% more often, consuming an extra 77 calories per day, on average.

Scientists believe that seeing food pushes you to consciously decide whether to eat it. Seeing it more often increases the chances you'll choose to eat the food.

Make this work in your favor by hiding tempting treats, while keeping healthy and nutritious food visible.

Keep tempting treats out of sight to prevent you from eating them mindlessly. On the other hand, keep healthy foods visible if hunger strikes.

6. Increase the inconvenience of eating

The more work is needed to eat a food, the less likely you are to eat it.

In one study, secretaries were given clear bowls of candy that were placed in three different spots around the office: on the desk, in a desk drawer, or 6 feet (1.8 meters) away from the desk.

Participants ate an average of 9 candies a day when the bowl was on the desk, 6 if the bowl was in the drawer, and 4 if they had to walk to get to the bowl.

When asked why they ended up eating less when the bowls were placed further away, participants stated that the extra distance gave them the time to think twice about whether they really wanted the candy.

Make this work for you by picking snacks that require some extra work or by keeping less nutritious snack foods out of reach.

Better yet, get in the habit of serving all foods on plates and eating only while sitting at the kitchen table.

This inconvenience might be just what you need to keep yourself from mindlessly snacking out of boredom or while preparing dinner.

Take the convenience out of eating. Adding extra steps will allow you to turn a mindless eating behavior into a conscious choice, reducing the chance of overindulgence.

7. Eat slowly

Slow eaters tend to eat less, feel fuller, and rate their meals as more pleasant than fast eaters.

Scientists believe that taking at least 20–30 minutes to finish a meal allows more time for your body to release hormones that promote feelings of fullness .

The extra time also allows your brain to realize you've eaten enough before you reach for that second serving.

Eating with your non-dominant hand or using chopsticks instead of a fork are two easy ways to reduce your eating speed and make this tip work for you. Chewing more often can help as well.

Slowing down your eating speed is an easy way to consume fewer calories and enjoy your meal more.

8. Choose your dining companions wisely

Eating with just one other person can push you to eat up to 35% more than when you eat alone. Eating with a group of 7 or more can further increase the amount you eat by 96%.

Scientists believe that this is especially true if you eat with family or friends, as it increases the time you spend eating, compared to when you eat by yourself.

The extra table time can push you to mindlessly nibble what's left on the plate while the rest of the group finishes their meal. It may also encourage you to eat a dessert you normally wouldn't.

Sitting next to slow eaters or people who normally eat less than you can work in your favor, influencing you to eat less or more slowly.

Other ways to counter this effect include choosing in advance how much of your meal you want to consume or asking the server to remove your plate as soon as you're done eating.

When dining in groups, sit next to people who eat less or at a slower pace than you. This can help prevent overeating.

9. Eat according to your inner clock

Relying on external cues like the time of day to determine your level of hunger may lead you to overeat.

A study demonstrated this idea by isolating participants in a windowless room with a clock as their only time cue. This clock was then artificially controlled to run faster.

Researchers noted that those who relied on the clock to know when to eat ended up eating more often than those who relied on internal hunger signals.

Interestingly, normal-weight participants were less likely to rely on the clock to determine whether it was time to eat.

If you have difficulty distinguishing physical from mental hunger, ask yourself whether you would readily eat an apple.

Remember, real hunger doesn't discriminate between foods.

Another telltale sign of mental hunger is wanting something specific, such as a BLT sandwich. A craving for a specific food is unlikely to indicate real hunger.

Rely on internal cues of hunger rather than external ones to decrease the likelihood of eating more than your body needs.

10. Beware of 'health foods'

Thanks to clever marketing, even foods labeled as healthy can push some people to mindlessly overeat.

"Low-fat" labels are a prime example, as foods low in fat are not necessarily low in calories. For instance, low-fat granola typically only has 10% fewer calories than regular-fat granola.

Nevertheless, study participants given granola labeled as "low-fat" ended up eating 49% more granola than those provided with the normally labeled granola.

Another study compared calorie intake from Subway and McDonald's. Those who ate at Subway consumed 34% more calories than they thought they did, while those who ate at McDonald's ate 25% more than they thought.

What's more, researchers noted that the Subway diners tended to reward themselves for their supposedly healthy meal choice by ordering chips or cookies with their meal.

This tendency to unconsciously overeat foods that are considered healthier, or compensate for them by having a side of something less healthy, is commonly known as the "health halo".

Steer clear of the effects of the health halo by picking items based on their ingredients rather than their health claims.

Also, remember to pay attention to the side items you choose.

Not all foods labeled as healthy are good for you. Focus on ingredients rather than health claims. Also, avoid picking unhealthy sides to accompany your healthy meal.

11. Don't stockpile

Research has shown that buying in bulk and stockpiling foods can push you to eat more.

A study investigated this effect by providing a group of normal-weight college students with four weeks of snacks. Some received a normal quantity of snacks, while others received double the amount.

Participants who received the doubled amount ate 81% more calories from snacks per week than those who received the normal quantity.

Avoid falling for this effect by purchasing only what is necessary and trying not to buy snack foods for future events or unexpected visits.

Finally, if you really must stockpile items, make sure to keep the extra items well out of eyesight.

Stockpiling foods increases your likelihood of overeating. Instead, get in the habit of buying only what is necessary for the week.

12. Maximize food volume

Eating large volumes of food tricks your brain into thinking you consumed more calories, helping decrease the likelihood of overeating and weight gain.

Researchers examined this effect by serving participants two smoothies identical in calories. However, one had air added to it. Those who drank the greater-volume smoothie felt fuller and ate 12% less at their next meal.

An easy way to add volume to your meals without increasing the calorie content is to pick high-fiber foods with a low calorie density, such as vegetables.

That's because extra fiber and water add volume, which stretches your stomach, helping you feel fuller.

Fiber also helps slow down the emptying rate of your stomach and can even stimulate the release of hormones that make you feel satisfied .

A good rule of thumb to maximize food volume is to fill at least half your plate with vegetables at each meal.

High-volume foods help you feel full and decrease food intake at the next meal. Eating fiber-rich foods is an easy way to do this.

13. Unplug while you eat

Eating while you're distracted can lead you to eat faster, feel less full, and mindlessly eat more.

Whether this is watching TV, listening to the radio, or playing a computer game, the type of distraction doesn't seem to matter much.

For instance, people watching television while eating their meals ate 36% more pizza and 71% more macaroni and cheese.

Plus, it seems that the longer the show, the more food you're likely to eat. One study noted that participants watching a 60-minute show ate 28% more popcorn than those enjoying a 30-minute show.

Notably, this effect seems to apply to nutritious foods as well as junk foods since participants watching the longer show also ate 11% more carrots.

Longer distractions extend the amount of time spent eating, making you more likely to overeat. In addition, eating while distracted may cause you to forget how much you've consumed, leading to overeating later in the day.

Indeed, another study observed that participants who played a computer game while eating lunch felt less full and snacked on nearly twice as many biscuits 30 minutes later, compared to their non-distracted counterparts.

By putting your phone away, switching off the TV, and focussing instead on the textures and flavors of your food, you'll quickly stop eating mindlessly and can instead enjoy your meal in a mindful manner.

Eating without using your TV, computer, or smartphone may help decrease the amount of food your body needs to feel full and satisfied.

The bottom line

To transition from mindless to mindful eating, try some of the simple tips above.

In doing so, you may improve your overall health and even lose weight in a way that feels easy and can be maintained over the long term.

For the best results, choose just three of these tips and aim to apply them consistently for around 66 days — the average time it takes to create a habit

WHAT'S THE DIFFERENCE BETWEEN INTUITIVE EATING AND MINDFUL EATING?

Before I started training in Intuitive Eating, I used the terms Mindful Eating and Intuitive Eating interchangeably. While this isn't totally incorrect, it's important to note the differences.

The Center for Mindful Eating defines mindful eating as "allowing yourself to become aware of the positive and nurturing opportunities that are available through food selection and preparation by respecting your own inner wisdom" and "using all your senses in choosing to eat food that is both satisfying to you and nourishing to your body and becoming aware of physical hunger and satiety cues to guide your decisions to begin and end eating."

You can tell right there that Intuitive Eating encompasses the principles of mindful eating. However it goes a step further, also addressing the importance of rejecting the dieting mentality, respecting your body (regardless of your weight or shape), coping with emotional eating, and gentle movement and nutrition without judgment. Both mindful eating and Intuitive Eating can be useful tools to help you reach a place of normal eating.

Are you interested in learning more about Intuitive Eating?

We work with clients virtually throughout the US, helping people who are frustrated with dieting change their relationship with food and say goodbye to diets once and for all. Learn more about our intuitive eating coaching programs to see how you can find balance and develop long-term lifestyle habits, no diets required.

Not ready for one-on-one coaching or looking to learn more about intuitive eating on your own? The Intuitive Eating Crash Course is a self-paced online course that walks you through the foundational principles of intuitive eating

CHAPTER 6

HOW TO PRACTICE INTUITIVE MOVEMENT

Movement is an important aspect in our day-to-day lives and it makes up the 9th principle of intuitive eating. The philosophy behind intuitive eating is applied to intuitive movement (referred to within this post interchangeably as intuitive exercise): listen to your body's cues to figure out what kind of movement or exercise would make you and your body feel good in that moment. In this post, we'll dive more in-depth about what intuitive movement is and I share tips on how to incorporate intuitive exercise into your life.

Many people approach exercise as something they "should do" or something to check off our to-do list. We know it's good for our health, yet it becomes something we either dread, force ourselves to do, or struggle to do it at all. Especially given how weight-focused and appearance-driven society, exercise becomes something we "have to" or "should do", instead of something we want to do. This is also why it is so hard for many people to start or maintain a consistent exercise practice.

What Is Intuitive Exercise/Movement?

Intuitive exercise, also known as intuitive movement, is the practice of connecting and listening to your body to figure out how it feels and what type of movement it needs that day. Instead of picking what type of exercise you think you "should" do, you use your body's internal cues to figure out the best type, length and intensity of the workout. Intuitive exercise also means that you are choosing to move your body for the sake of self-care or health benefits (see below), instead of doing it to lose weight or burn calories.

To get started with intuitive movement, ask yourself questions like: "What does my body need today?", "What type of movement do I feel like doing?", or "What type of exercise would be most beneficial to my body today?". Some days this may mean you do an intense spin class, while other days it may mean restorative yoga or a short walk. Intuitive movement is flexible, not rigid, and gives you the space to explore what feels good in your body.

Instead of exercising to burn calories or lose weight, it's about exercising because of the positive health and mood benefits you see. Instead of forcing yourself to do X days of cardio and X days of weight-training, you get to explore movement that feels good in your body. This shift in mindset allows exercise to become more enjoyable, less stressful and ends up being something to look forward to, rather than dread. Practicing intuitive movement can help you nurture a healthier relationship with exercise and your body.

Health Benefits of Intuitive Movement

The benefits of exercise are well-established. But unfortunately, much of the time people are told to exercise with the main purpose of burning calories, losing weight, or compensating for what they eat. These types of extrinsic motivation get old quickly – when the results aren't what you expect, or it's taking too long to get results, many people just give up and stop exercising. Intuitive movement, on the other hand, puts the focus on internal or intrinsic motivation. You think of using movement as a form of self-care, instead of punishment, and shift your focus to the health benefits your body experiences, such as:

- Improved sleep
- Lower levels of stress and anxiety
- Increased energy
- Improved mood
- Higher bone density
- Increased muscle mass
- Better balance and flexibility
- Reduced risk of heart disease, type 2 diabetes, high blood pressure and high cholesterol
- Increased memory and mental clarity
- Reduction in chronic pain (for some people)

Tips to Practice Intuitive Movement

1. Do a quick body scan.

A short body scan is a great way to begin tuning into your body's physical and emotional state. It takes less than a minute and can even be done while you are lying in bed after you wake up. Starting at the top of your head, focus on each of your body parts and how they are feeling. Head, neck, shoulders, arms, chest, back, etc – making your way slowly down your body. This will help you figure out how your body is feeling that day – whether it is tight and sore, stressed and wound up, or loose and energized.

2. Avoid rigid structure and all-or-nothing thinking.

When you try to keep a strict exercise routine it can mean that, if it doesn't happen, you end up feeling guilty which can cause more stress and lower motivation to exercise the next time. Intuitive exercise is flexible, so if you end up missing a workout, you show yourself some compassion, be understanding for why you couldn't make it to the gym, and then move on. Research shows that self-compassion is linked to increased motivation and improved health behaviors so in the long run, this can actually help you maintain a consistent exercise routine. Similar to intuitive meal planning, intuitive exercise can have a loose structure to maintain somewhat of a plan while still having flexibility. This can look different for everyone and can even change week to week. For me, there are some weeks that I pencil in a few gym days and/or yoga sessions into my calendar then see how I feel that day. Then there are other weeks that I don't make any plan at all, but ask myself each morning "Do

I feel like doing any exercise or movement today?" and, if yes, "What would feel good today?"

3. Choose a form of movement or exercise that you enjoy.

There is no reason to do exercise that you dislike! If you find yourself dreading your workout, it's a sign that you're probably not engaging in forms of movement that makes you or your body happy. Try to figure out what brings you the most joy and what feels the best for your body. If you can't think of any types of movement that you like doing, then it's time for some exploration and trial and error. Look into different classes, whether it's in person classes (think yoga, pilates, kickboxing, ballroom dancing, spin class, water aerobics, belly dancing, etc) or online streaming workouts or videos. Or get outside and try hiking, biking, walking, jogging, or – in the winter – cross-country skiing or snowshoeing.

4. Pay attention to how the movement makes you feel.

Check in with yourself after you finish exercising – how does your body feel? Did your workout or movement that day leave you feeling energized? Do you feel stronger or have less pain? Focus on the internal, intrinsic benefits that you notice. Note: if you're feeling extremely fatigued and drained after your workout, this is a sign that you've either overworked and pushed your body too far and that you may need a rest day.

5. Think about your "why".

Listen for that voice that pops up in your head when you think about exercise or movement. Are you exercising because you think you "should" or because you want to lose weight or because you want to burn calories? Notice when those "shoulds" pop-up and get curious about it. Then focus on finding a reason to move your body that has nothing to do with weight loss or calories. This could be for the way it makes you feel, for the physical health or mental benefits, or because you know it will help you get a good nights sleep. Reframe exercise as something that you are doing / can do to take care of your body (rather than punish it).

6. Do not be afraid of rest days.

Rest days are just as important as active days, as they allow your body to recover and heal. When you begin to strengthen your interoceptive awareness skills and build up body trust, you learn to accept whatever it is your body needs that day. Trust that when your body needs a rest day, it needs a rest day.

7. Invest in comfortable clothing.

No one likes feeling uncomfortable in what they're wearing – it leaves you feeling insecure and even alters your mood. Clothing matters – purchase some fun, cute, comfortable workout clothes that you feel good in. Check out brands that offer a wide range of sizes, like Girlfriend Collective (up to 6XL), Superfit Hero (up to 5XL), Target's The Joy Lab Line (up to 4XL), K-Deer (up to 4XL), Fabletics (up to 3XL), Good American (up to 4XL), Dear

Kate (up to 3XL) and Knix sports bras (that include F & G cups).

CHAPTER 7

INTUITIVE EATING WITH FOOD ALLERGIES OR SENSITIVIES

When learning about intuitive eating you will often hear 'listen to your body', 'make peace with all foods' and 'all foods can fit'. These phrases may not resonate if you have food allergies, food intolerances or need to follow a medically-necessary diet. But there are ways in which you can practice and incorporate intuitive eating with food allergies or sensitivities. Brenna breaks it down for you here.

Some of the language used in intuitive eating may make it seem like it's not something you can do if you have food allergies, intolerances or sensitivities. On top of this, diet culture and people who sell diets have co-opted the language of medically-necessary diets, like those for food allergies. They've repackaged them as fad or trend diets (i.e. anyone on a gluten-free diet who doesn't have an intolerance to gluten, they're doing this because "gluten-free' has become a fad diet), which can make you feel like you're not being taken seriously, when you need to ensure the safety of foods you eat.

But in fact, intuitive eating can work perfectly well even if you have food allergies or sensitivities. In fact, the principles of intuitive eating can be really supportive in helping you create a more peaceful relationship with food – aka not feeling obsessive – while catering to any allergies or intolerances that you may have.

This is something we help clients with and is something that I've personally had to navigate as well. Celiac Disease is very common in my family and I've adopted a gluten-free diet since early high school. In my own experience, I've found that it can be tough to manage the feelings that come from needing to avoid certain ingredients or foods, and pay extra attention to what I'm eating, while also trying not to follow food rules or feel obsessed about what I eat.

Intuitive Eating with Food Allergies: Flexibility is Key

Food allergies can be traumatic and have a lasting impact on your relationship with food and your body. You may have had an allergic reaction, visited many doctors, done multiple tests, felt sick and confused as you teased out what foods were causing your symptoms. All of these experiences can create a disconnect and distrust in your body. Creating a flexible eating environment doesn't mean making yourself unsafe or ignoring your allergy. Instead, it means liberalizing other areas of your diet to minimize stress and re-establish eating as an enjoyable experience. Having the flexibility to find foods you enjoy that still fit with your dietary needs both keep you safe but also prevents you from feeling too restricted or stressed around food choices and availability.

Step 1: Reframe Your Intention

A helpful place to start is to reframe how you think about your food allergy or dietary restriction. Shift the perspective from a 'diet' relating to weight or physical appearance, to whatever reason this food doesn't feel good or work well with your body. Rather than thinking of it as a rule reminiscent of dieting or restriction, think about it as a choice informed by your experience with this food or knowledge of how this food doesn't react well in your body.

For example, shift the intention from "because I'm not allowed to have that food" to "I choose foods that make me feel good" which in this case are foods that are free of _____.

Setting this intention behind your way of eating can act as a grounding reminder when you feel challenged by diet culture or diet messaging – you're working with your body, not against it.

Step 2: Move From Scarcity to Abundance

The messages used around intuitive eating of 'spend less time thinking about food' or 'no food rules' can feel foreign when you actually do need to pay special attention to what you're eating. It can also make you feel left out if certain traditional dishes, holiday meals or group gatherings are centered around foods that you need to avoid.

Practice shifting your mindset from scarcity to abundance. Rather than focusing on all the things you can't have, think about how you can make as many foods as possible available. For example, using food substitutes, introducing friends to your allergen-free options and choosing restaurants that have allergen-friendly dishes. You can also think of it as an opportunity to create new dishes, experiment with substitutes and find foods that are satisfying and nourishing that also fit your needs.

This is where that extra thought and planning around meals can be beneficial and ultimately offer more flexibility and inclusivity.

- Find ways to still have your favorite foods and make safe foods enjoyable. Food allergies are inherently restrictive so allowing yourself to enjoy your favorite foods in an allergen-free version can minimize the feeling of being restricted. Use spices, sauces, or spreads to make your allergen-friendly food taste good, and experiment with different recipes or new products. Free of allergens doesn't mean your meals need to be free of flavor or satisfaction.

- Food allergies and intolerances are where food substitutes shine! Allowing yourself the flexibility to have and try different substitutes like gluten-free bagels or dairy-free ice creams can help you feel less restricted around food – and remind you that you aren't on a 'diet' you're choosing foods that feel good for you. Especially in our dieting society this is an important reminder that you're not avoiding (bagels, pizza, ice cream, nutty desserts), you're avoiding the allergen but can still enjoy those foods, allergen-free.

Step 3: How to Handle the Increased Food Talk

Another aspect of food allergies/medical diets is that it can increase the talk around food, from friends, strangers, family, etc. If your allergy/intolerance is often found in foods that society deems 'unhealthy' you may receive increased comments around why you're not eating that food or how you're 'being so good' for choosing another option. These comments are unwarranted and can be even more frustrating because they dismiss the intention behind your choices – to choose foods that are enjoyable and safe to you, not to be on 'another diet'. Here are some more resources and tips on how to handle food and diet talk.

A Few Other Things to Keep in Mind:

1. Allow yourself to have substitutes and fun foods. A gluten-free bagel is not the same as a fresh NY bagel, but ordering one or having them in the freezer so that you can be included when friends or family have bagels with breakfast can make your diet feel less like you're restricted. This can also help you focus on the people around you rather than the food itself. Keep allergen-free foods in the house, including tasty, satisfying options. Allergen-free doesn't need to mean boring or bland, you still deserve fun foods just because they taste good. This is where gentle nutrition and #allfoodsfit still applies.

2. Remember that ensuring your food is safe is not annoying or unreasonable. Whether that means asking your server to double-check if a dish is

allergen-free, or bringing an extra snack in case what's served isn't allergen-safe. Your safety and peace of mind is a priority and should be respected.

Bottom Line: Eating is Individual

It makes sense that one way of eating wouldn't work for every person. All of our bodies are different – as are our food preferences, access to foods, schedules, culinary skills, etc – regardless of allergies, autoimmune issues, and intolerances. Each of these issues is complex and in terms of figuring out how food can fit into helping with symptom management – there can be an overwhelming amount of information, and unfortunately, many anecdotal suggestions of elimination/restriction.

This can make it tricky to pick apart what is someone's lived experience of 'what worked for them' vs. what might work for you – or be realistic/known to be helpful. Messages with the promise to 'cure' or 'heal' – this language is sometimes a red flag that a program may be 'overpromising'. You are the expert of your body but with so many layers to food allergies and intolerances, or with people who have a more complex health history, it can be helpful to have the support of a trained professional

CHAPTER 8

HOW TO RAISE AN INTUITIVE EATER

"If we gave him that bag, he would eat the whole thing!" I recently heard a friend of mine say about his kiddo when he saw my six-year-old take the bag of Doritos. He then told his child he had to eat his lunch first if he wanted a chip. This might not seem like a bad idea. In fact, it sounds healthy. Eat some nutrient dense foods and then you can have a little bit of "junk food", kind of like the 80/20 rule. And while I don't normally give my kids a bag of Doritos to walk around with, we were camping, and he grabbed it. And it honestly just wasn't a big deal, because I am raising him to be an intuitive eater who trusts himself with food.

How Do I Raise An Intuitive Eater?

It is essential to give children the opportunity to make food decisions and learn from them without judgement. Parents provide the what, when, and where of food, and children decide how much to eat, if anything. There is no pressure or force involved. When children are presented with this variety in a neutral environment, they are more likely to expand their intake.

I am all about creating the opportunity for children to have variety and be presented with nutritious foods. In fact, that's how I normally offer food. I provide a selection, including carbohydrates, protein, fat, produce, and sometimes a fun food (chips, cookies, candy, etc.) But there is no requirement to eat certain things or in a certain order.

What is your child hearing when you make food rules?

The message, "You need to eat this in order to eat that," creates the potential for more harm than good. I absolutely understand this thought process. We are all trying to do the best for our children and want to raise happy, healthy, and competent eaters. So, if this is you, please pour yourself a cup of compassion and know you are doing your best. Then take a second, and read into the messages that your kids might be hearing:

- "Sandwiches, fruits, and veggies are good. Chips are bad."

- "You cannot make your own food choices."

- "Don't listen to your body. Instead, follow the rules."

- "It doesn't matter how hungry you are, if you want chips you have to eat MORE food."

- "Cookies are a reward for doing something good. You deserve them."

Unfortunately, focusing on the external messaging around food, takes away from the ability to eat based on internal cues, which is the key for raising an intuitive eater.

What's more important… the food or relationship?

While some of these messages might sound balanced, it's because of the lens we are hearing them through. We are constantly bombarded with statistics about our poor health and dietary habits. So, it makes sense we are scared our children will develop Type 2 Diabetes, high cholesterol, or become "obese". Yet, the rate of eating disorders in our youth far surpasses the rate of any of these conditions.

Further, early dieting behaviors are associated with binge eating and the development of all types of eating disorders, yet intuitive eating is associated with a decreased risk of these behaviors. Therefore, the RELATIONSHIP with food is more important than the food itself!

Common Pitfalls to Avoid:

When I have this conversation with parents, they often believe their child is different. They believe they must control the food and set limits about portions. Once we dig a little deeper, we always find one or more underlying issues.

Not offering "fun foods" regularly. As parents we often believe "fun foods" should be given sparingly. So, it might feel like you are offering them regularly. But when I talk to parents, it often turns out they are giving them less frequently than they realize, and it might feel restrictive to the kiddos. If there is a food in question, offer it daily!

Having a history of restriction. If a food has been off limits or given sparingly in the past, it will likely take awhile before your child starts to trust it will be offered again and again. They may have an underlying fear it will go away and feel they need to eat as much as possible right now. Stick with it and keep offering it!

Making comments or judgments. Be mindful of your language around foods. When we use terms like good, bad, healthy, unhealthy, and "junk" foods, we create the idea that we shouldn't eat them. Food feels more desirable when it appears to be off limits. When you are not offering cookies, you don't have to say, because they are "unhealthy". Instead, simply say, "They're not available right now! We'll have them soon!"

Acting like it's a novelty. Are you serving the food consistently but making a big deal about it? Maybe you say excitedly, "We're having a treat tonight!" It's wonderful to enjoy foods, but a lot of hype around them will give them more power. Ice cream is delicious but so are yogurt and fruit. Treat dessert foods with the same energy you treat all other foods!

Having your own energy about the food and the way you eat it. Children learn more from our actions than what we tell them. When you eat a bag of chips and make a comment that you can't stop, or someone should take them away from you, you are sending the message people can't be trusted with food. Or if you don't keep certain foods in the house because you are scared you will eat them all, your children will pick up on this. If you are struggling, seek additional support for yourself!

Conclusion

Children are natural born intuitive eaters. They can internally regulate their intake. Our job as parents is to nurture that relationship and reinforce, they can TRUST themselves. There are times when they may eat the whole bag of cookies, and that's OK. What's more important is how we react and what they learn. If you struggle to adopt this mentality, you may want to examine your own beliefs and behaviors around food. Give the process some time. As parents, we are feeding for the future and helping our children develop their own skills to become competent eaters long after we are there to control the food. With a few tweaks, patience, and trust, you too can raise an intuitive eater

STEPS TO BECOME AN INTUITIVE EATER

Ready to learn how to start intuitive eating? Begin by following these helpful intuitive eating tips:

1. **Acknowledge That Quick-Fix Or Fad Diets Don't Work**

It's tempting to believe there's a way to lose weight quickly, easily and permanently by taking drastic measures, eliminating entire food groups, radically cutting calories or going on a low-carb diet. But in reality, most people can't override their body's natural biology and cravings for extended periods of time. Instead of trying diet after diet only to feel like a failure every time you "fall off the wagon," stop dieting all together.

Give up the idea that there's new and better diets lurking around the corner and return to what has worked for people for centuries: eating real foods, practicing moderation and moving your body! Aim for a nutrient-dense diet that supports a healthy body, stable mind and steady energy levels, all without trying to be "perfect."

Make food choices that honor your health and satisfy your taste buds, while also making you feel good. If you're not exactly sure which foods work best for you, and which may not, consider using an intuitive eating workbook to track your reactions to different foods, or perhaps work with a trained intuitive eating coach.

2. Fuel Yourself with Enough Calories

The motivation of simply wanting to lose weight to look better, especially for a specific event, can be temporary and fleeting — but even more importantly, it causes many people to deprive themselves of enough calories and rest, which has damaging effects on the metabolism. Recognize that it's important to give your body the calories it needs, otherwise you're likely to deal with feelings of chronic fatigue, deprivation and resentment, plus you have the urge to overeat or binge eat due to biological changes.

3. Avoid "Good/Bad" or "Black/White" Thinking About Certain Foods

It's true that some foods are more nutrient-dense than others, but vowing to 100 percent eliminate certain foods or food groups from your diet forever can just increase stress and feelings of preoccupation with "forbidden foods."

Intuitive eaters aim to "make peace with food, call a truce and stop the food fight." Of course, you want to prioritize eating all types of healthy foods over highly processed foods, but don't expect perfection and assume you'll never have your favorite comfort foods again.

If you tell yourself you can't or shouldn't have a particular food ever again, it can lead to intense feelings of shame along with uncontrollable cravings. Experts believe that all-or-nothing thinking about foods can increase the likelihood for bingeing, because when someone finally "gives in" to their forbidden food, they are then tempted to eat very large amounts, to feel like it's their "last chance" and then to feel overwhelming guilt.

Remember that it's what you eat consistently over time that matters and that "progress, not perfection" is the goal. Try your best not to view certain foods (or entire food groups like carbohydrates, fats or animal proteins, for example) as "bad." Instead, just aim to have them less often and focus your attention on adding in more of the things that support your health and make you feel good.

4. Learn to Eat When You're Hungry, and Stop When Full

"Feeling your fullness" and "honoring your hunger" are two key principles of intuitive eating. Many people find that when they don't categorize any foods as totally off-limits or deprive themselves of enough calories, they can finally start to eat in line with what their body really needs.

5. Find Ways to Handle Stress and Emotions without the Use Of Food

For many people, IE opens the doors to finding new ways to destress, comfort, nurture or distract themselves, and resolve emotional issues, without overeating or turning to comfort food. We all feel tough emotions from time to time like frustration, anxiety, loneliness or boredom, but it's important to realize that food can't actually fix any of these feelings or solve problems in your life.

Emotional eating might feel good in the moment, but it actually usually winds up making the initial problem even worse, because then you have to deal with feelings of shame or discomfort, too. Wondering how to be happier everyday and to find appropriate outlets for uncomfortable emotions and stress? Try exercising in a fun way, meditation or healing prayer, writing a journal, massage therapy, acupuncture or spending time with people you love.

When it comes to learning how to cope with stress in a healthy manner, many people can also benefit from keeping an intuitive eating journal or using an intuitive eating app for support, such as YouAte. These are helpful for becoming more aware of unhealthy habits, of what you're eating and why and of how you feel before and after you eat. For example, you may choose to write down what you ate, how you felt, how hungry you were, how full you were after and your feelings regarding different eating experiences. According to a 2019 pilot study that is investigating the use of smartphone apps for learning IE, engaging in these types of practices is believed to help "bridge the gap between intentions to perform a particular behavior and the actual behavioral change."

6. Practice Body Acceptance and Be Realistic About Your Goals

We all have unique genetic blueprints, and for many people, reaching their "ideal weight" is unrealistic, unsustainable and possibly even unhealthy. Just because you're carrying around a little extra weight than you'd like to doesn't necessarily mean you're unhealthy and that you need to force yourself to be smaller.

Ask yourself if your goals are realistic. Are you setting the bar too high? Is your current diet or exercise routine causing more stress and harm than it's worth? Are you accepting of your natural body or constantly fighting your genetics and beating yourself up? Respect your body, drop the guilt as much as you can, and start feeling better about who you are so you can take better care of yourself long-term.

How Do You Raise an Intuitive Eater?

Principles of intuitive eating can benefit children and parents alike, as eating intuitively builds autonomy and self-trust. A highly-regarded specialist in children's eating named Ellyn Satter even created the Feeding Dynamics Model (or "division of responsibility in feeding") in the early 1980s to help parents raise intuitive eaters. In this model, the parent or caregiver provides structure by choosing what food to serve at regular meal and snack times, while the child decides how much of the foods offered to eat. The goal is to allow children to remain sensitive to internal hunger and satiety cues and to avoid disrupting the child's ability to self-regulate energy intake and the amount of food eaten.

According to an article published by Today's Dietician Magazine, "Allowing kids to eat intuitively gives children a greater sense of self-esteem, understanding of boundaries [and] connection to family and caregivers during meals, and typically they will enjoy a wider variety of foods … while strategies such as encouraging, bribing or tricking may be well-intentioned, they end up increasing picky eating and escalating power struggles at the table."

According to dietitians trained in IE for children, the best thing parents can do when feeding their children is to not say anything once the food is in front of the child, but rather to focus on offering nutritionally-complete snacks and meals that provide at least two of the three macronutrients. This is said to "help promote stable moods and blood sugar, helping kids and parents hone in on true hunger and fullness. Many experts also recommend eating as a family at the table, without devices or other distractions.

Precautions/Side Effects

How do you start intuitive eating if you have a history of disordered eating or a complicated relationship with food? The best thing to do in this situation is seek out help from an intuitive eating counselor, who may be a registered dietician, therapist or health coach who has received an intuitive eating certification.

This is especially important if you've struggled with an eating disorder in the past, as IE tends to bring up a lot of difficult feelings and can be hard to navigate on your own during different stages of recovery from eating disorders. One reason that IE can be tough during recovery is because hunger/fullness cues tend to be unreliable for a period of time as the body adjusts. During early stages of recovery, meal plans are often necessary to help with weight restoration, re-nourishing the body and establishing normalized eating patterns, but after some time, IE can become more of a focus.

It's recommended that those who struggle with eating-related issues first read the official Intuitive Eating book and/or buy the official Intuitive Eating Workbook to help themselves learn more. It's also recommended they find a therapist or dietitian who truly understands this work and how it should be implemented during recovery.

Final Thoughts

- What is intuitive eating? One definition of intuitive eating (IE) is, "trusting your inner body wisdom to make choices around food that feel good in your body, without judgment and without influence from diet culture."

- Here's how to practice intuitive eating: follow the 10 principles of intuitive eating as described by authors of the Intuitive Eating book, some of which include: reject the diet mentality, honor your hunger, make peace with food, challenge the food police, discover the satisfaction factor and honor your feelings without using food.

- Keep in mind that weight loss is not necessarily how you should judge your intuitive eating results. While weight loss may occur, it isn't the primary benefit or goal. The real benefits of IE include lowered stress, more flexibility, eating a wide variety of foods, better self-trust, increased confidence and improved overall health.

INTUITIVE EATER EXPERIENCE: THINGS I LEARNED DURING MY FIRST WEEK OF INTUITIVE EATING

Health and wellness touch each of us differently. This is one person's story.

I'm a chronic dieter.

I first started restricting my calorie intake in junior high, and I've been on some kind of diet ever since. I've tried low-carb diets, calorie counting, tracking my macros, keto, and Whole30. I've committed to increasing my exercise and eating less more times than I can count.

After nearly two decades of basically nonstop restriction, I've learned that I almost always gain the weight back. Dieting also creates a lot of negativity in my life, damaging my relationship with my body and food.

I feel anxious about my body and anxious about what I eat. I often find myself overeating when presented with "off-limits" foods and feeling guilty about it far too often.

I've been familiar with intuitive eating for some time, but it wasn't until I started following a registered dietitian on social media who's an advocate for the practice that I realized it might be able to help me step away from diet culture.

Intuitive eating provides a framework for an emotionally and physically healthy way of life by asking people to listen to their body as they make decisions about what they eat and how much. Although intuitive eating is based in making personal choices about food, it's a bit more complicated than eating whatever you want.

Intuitive eating also pushes for acceptance of body diversity, eating based on cues from the body instead of cues from diet culture, and movement for enjoyment instead of for the purpose of weight loss.

On their website, the founders of the practice outline ten guiding principles for intuitive eating that help shed light on his way of life. Here's an overview:

- Break up with dieting with the understanding that years of following diet culture takes time to correct. This means no calorie counting and no off-limits foods. It also means you have permission to eat whatever you want.

- Eat when you're hungry and stop when you're full. Trust your body and the cues it sends you instead of relying on external cues like a calorie count to tell you to stop eating.

- Eat for satisfaction. Place value in food tasting good, rather than food being low-calorie or low-carb.

- Honor your emotions. If food has been used to cover up, suppress, or comfort difficult emotions, it's time to let in the discomfort of those emotions and focus on using food for its intended purposes — nourishment and satisfaction.

- Move because it makes you feel good and brings you joy, not as a formula for burning calories or making amends for eating high-calorie food.

- Gently follow basic nutrition guidelines such as eating more vegetables and eating whole grains.

Everything I Learned During 10 Days Of Intuitive Eating

I committed to 10 days of practicing intuitive eating with the hope that this practice would become a part of the rest of my life. Here's a look at all the things I learned during my time with intuitive eating and how I hope to move forward.

1. I love rice

I'm a previous ketogenic dieter and rice has been off-limits for me multiple times throughout my life. Not anymore!

By lunchtime of the first day of this challenge, I wanted a bowl of rice loaded with sautéed veggies, a fried egg, and soy sauce. When day two rolled around, I wanted it again. Throughout the entire 10 days of eating intuitively, I was a little fixated on certain foods that used to be off-limits and it was honestly really fun to follow those cravings without guilt. I'm not sure if this is because my body really wanted rice, or if this was a side effect of so much restriction in the past.

2. Eating good food is fun

One pleasant surprise from days three and four were my cravings for some foods I normally associate with dieting. There's a specific chocolate protein powder I love but have always included in a meal plan for a diet. A few days into living a diet-free life, I found myself wanting to have a smoothie because it sounded good, not because it was a part of my meal plan.

The important thing about gentle nutrition is that it doesn't mean you remove other foods suddenly. You can make daily food choices that're satisfying and feel right without getting extremely restrictive about other foods.

3. My hunger signals are a mess

By day two, one thing became very clear — years of restricting followed by overindulgence and overeating has completely jacked up my hunger signals. Eating food I like was fun, but knowing when I was actually hungry and when I was satisfied was incredibly challenging over the course of the entire 10 days.

Some days, I'd stop eating and realize ten minutes later I was still hungry. Other days, I wouldn't realize I had overeaten until it was too late and I felt miserable. I think this is a learning process, so I kept trying to be gracious with myself. I'm choosing to believe that, with time, I'll learn to listen to my body and feed it well.

4. I'm not ready for body acceptance yet

This might be the hardest lesson I'm learning during this experience with intuitive eating. Even though I can see the value of accepting my body as it is, it isn't really sinking in for me yet. If I'm being perfectly honest, I still want to be thin.

On day five, I experienced a significant amount of anxiety about not weighing myself and had to hop on the scale before I went on with the rest of my day. I hope that with time being a specific size will be less of a priority to me.

On day six, I spent time writing in my journal about how I feel about the people I'm close to, noting that what I value about them has nothing to do with their size. My hope is that I'll learn to feel the same way about myself soon.

5. Special days are triggering AF

During this 10-day experiment, I celebrated my anniversary with my husband and went on a weekend trip with my family. It was no surprise to me that I felt really vulnerable and anxious about food during these special days.

In the past, celebrating has always meant either denying myself of any "special" foods and feeling miserable or overindulging in special foods and feeling guilty.

Navigating special days on intuitive eating wasn't easy. In fact, it went really poorly. I still overate and felt guilty about what I ate when it was all said and done.

I think this is one of those things that's going to take time to figure out. Hopefully, once I really get a handle on giving myself unconditional permission to eat, these days will feel less anxiety-ridden.

6. I'm bored

Afternoons often become a time of mindless snacking for me. Committing to only eating when I'm hungry meant that I kept noticing I was bored and lonely during the afternoons. My kids were napping or having their screen time and I felt like I was just wandering the house looking for something to do.

I think that the solution to this is two-fold. I do think I need to learn to be more comfortable with not filling every moment with fun but I also believe I haven't done a great job at making time for enjoyable, fulfilling activities. I'm working on picking up a book more often, listening to podcasts, and writing for fun during these lulls in my afternoon.

7. This is going to take time, and maybe even therapy

By days nine and ten, it was pretty obvious that this experiment is just the tip of the iceberg. Nearly 20 years entrenched in diet culture can't be erased by 10 days of intuitive eating and that's fine with me.

I'm also open to the idea that I might not be able to do this alone. It was a therapist who first mentioned intuitive eating to me and I might revisit this idea with her in the future. Overall, I'm prepared for this to take a lot of work and healing on my part — but freedom from the hamster wheel of dieting is worth it to me.

CHAPTER 9

CAN INTUITIVE EATING HELP YOU ACHIEVE THE BODY YOU WANT?

Intuitive eating isn't a new concept. In fact, it's probably been around for centuries. It just so happens some bright spark has decided to put a fancy label on it. Cynically, I'd say that's to sell you something. But hey, I could be wrong (although that's never happened before).

Whether you realise it or not, your body has inbuilt hunger and fullness sensors.

No doubt you've had feelings of hunger in the past. ██████, all the ██████ time, am I right?

This is largely to do with hormones in the body.

The Role Of Leptin And Ghrelin

Leptin and Ghrelin are both hormones playing a role in hunger and satiety (the feeling of fullness). If Ghrelin is high and Leptin is low, you feel hungry. Conversely, if Leptin is high and Ghrelin is low, you feel full and satisfied.

Improving hormonal balance and optimising your health is largely achieved through proper weight management and a healthier lifestyle. Simply put, you still need to focus on a calorie deficit and making more nutritious food choices.

So with all that said, where does intuitive eating come into play?

The concept of intuitive eating encourages you you use your natural hunger and fullness cues to regulate how much you eat. No foods are restricted (I like the sound of that). And you can eat what you want, when you want, as long as you listen to those pesky hormones.

This all sounds great in theory, but it does have its pitfalls. And that's especially true if you're someone who has struggled with weight loss.

The Downside Of Intuitive Eating

Ultimately, a form of intuitive eating is what we should all be striving for.

Whether you agree or disagree with intuitive eating, it's hard to argue that the core principles aren't something we should all adopt to some degree. After all, there aren't many people on the plant who want to manage calories and live on MyFitnessPal for the rest of their lives.

But intuitive eating isn't easy. In fact, you can get it massively wrong if you don't know what you're doing.

The 3 Cons Of Intuitive Eating

1. Intuitive eating is a learned skill. It requires a good understanding of food, calories, portion sizes, and basic nutrition. It takes time to understand what foods are calorie dense and should be eaten in lower quantities. Expecting you to get all of this right from

day one is a tall order. And let's face it...you'll probably get it wrong.

2. Less structure and guidelines. If you're a beginner, having a basic structure and guidelines to follow is particularly important. But that doesn't mean you have to calorie count. You just need to know what you're doing is helping create that deficit.

3. Easy to overeat. Nuts, avocado, and foods such as these are full of nutrients and considered healthy. But they also contain a ██t load of calories and aren't great and helping you feel full. So the novice intuitive eater could easily eat may too many calories, while not feeling very full. This means your calorie deficit could be well and truly ██████ from the get go.

The Upside Of Intuitive Eating

So with all that said, you might be forgiven for thinking I'm against intuitive eating. But you couldn't be more wrong. In fact, it's an approach I encourage all of my online coaching clients to progress towards. I call it "Coaching To Live."

Coaching to live is about helping you feel comfortable managing your weight without the constant need for calorie monitoring. It's designed to enable you to live a leaner, healthier life for good. Because achieving a 12 week transformation is great. But maintaining it for life is the real goal, right?

Clients, such as Emily (in the picture below) are testament to the approach. Achieving and maintaining an awesome transformation, without being glued to MyFitnessPal forever. And you can see more transformations just like hers right here.

So, if you're in the right stage of your body transformation journey, intuitive eating could be the perfect strategy for you. Here's some of the key benefits it offers.

The 3 Pros Of Intuitive Eating

- Reduces Hang Ups About Certain Foods. There are no restrictions on what you can eat. So the demonisation of food doesn't exist, which is great. Ultimately, intuitive eating is a sign of having a great relationship with food. You just have to remember to keep things under control.

- Less structure and guidelines. This was a con, but it's also a pro. Because once you have the basics of nutrition in place, not having rules is liberating. You can fly the nutritional nest and soar like a nutrition eagle.

- Be healthy and enjoy life. Let's face it, when you're in a dieting phase you don't live life to the absolute full. Yes, you can enjoy great food and still lose weight. But you're putting a certain degree of limitation on your diet...you have to. But intuitive eating allows you to be a little more 'free and easy' with your food choices.

TIPS TO TRANSITION FROM CALORIE COUNTER TO INTUITIVE EATER

While intuitive eating might not be the place for you to start, it might be a great place to end up. So that begs the question, "how do you transition to be am intuitive eater?"

And that's a great question, so here's 7 top tips to make that transition as smooth as silk.

1. Start With Habit Changes

If you're an absolute beginner to nutrition, then you don't even need to jump straight to calorie counting, let alone intuitive eating. Adopting positive eating habits that promote a calorie deficit are a great place to start. For example, eating 200g of green vegetables with lunch and dinner, removing starchy carbs from one main meal, and having a portion of protein with each meal are all great examples.

2. Progress To A More Structured Approach

It's possible you might find a habit based approach lacks a little precision. And you might want to try a more targeted approach. So this is where calorie tracking may be a good option. Of course you don't have to calorie count, there are lots of other ways to approach dieting. But just remember, you need to create that calorie deficit.

3. Practice Mindful Meal Planning

As you figure out what to eat each day, week, and month consciously think about adding more low calorie, nutritious foods into your diet. These types of foods can help with feelings of satiety. So getting used to incorporating these foods at an early stage will certainly help when you come to start intuitive eating.

4. Practice Mindful Eating

You and I live in a world where everything is fast-paced right down to how quickly we can shovel food into our faces. But mindful eating can be a great way to avoid eating a bunch of calories without even realising it. So take time to eat your meals and chew each bite fully.

5. Take Mental Notes Of Portions

If you're going to spend a good chunk of your life tracking calories and weighing food then don't do it blindly. Instead, look at what 100g of chicken looks like and how much of the plate your 150g of cooked rice takes up. Further down the line, this makes it much easier to intuitively eat and stay on track.

6. Take Your Time

Learning these intuitive eating skills might take time. So don't expect to be an expert overnight. Transition slowly and when the time is right as you build up your knowledge.

7. Be Like The Chameleon

You can switch between dieting methods any time you choose. Don't feel like you're stuck with one way of eating forever if it doesn't suit your goal at the time. So if you feel like you need to tighten up your nutrition for bit, switch from intuitive eating back to tracking. And when you're done, switch back again. Make everything fit you.

For most, intuitive eating is the end and not the start of the journey.

Intuitive eating is a great approach to eating. But it requires a level of skill and nutritional knowledge. In my opinion, this makes it something to progress towards, rather than the approach adopted from day one.

Work on getting the basics in place, start making progress, and then transition as you become more confident.

CHAPTER 10

TIPS FOR PRACTICING INTUITIVE EATING DURING PREGNANCY

Intuitive eating, or mindful eating, is the practice of learning to pay attention to (and honoring) your body's natural cues in regards to food.

This means nourishing your body when it's hungry, noticing and stopping when you're full, and honoring your cravings.

And when you're pregnant? All of the above can be especially difficult.

It's time for some real talk, friends. Pregnancy is hard.

We don't have to tell you that we live in a culture of constant pressures around food, weight, and body image. We're constantly being pushed to compare ourselves to one another, when we all know that nothing positive comes out of doing that.

For this reason and others, pregnancy can be an incredibly challenging season. Intuitive eating is a great habit to learn and practice, especially when eating for two. Research shows that intuitive eating can have very positive impacts on a woman's mental health.

Here are a few ways to start incorporating intuitive eating into your pregnancy journey.

Tips For Practicing Intuitive Eating During Pregnancy

1. Make peace with food and your body.

Many of us have experienced a challenging relationship with food at one point or another, and pregnancy can bring this to the forefront and amplify it. Make the decision to stop any negative self talk that may be lurking. The fact is, pregnancy means that you're going to look, feel, eat, and move differently – and that's okay! In fact, it's totally normal. It's also temporary.

This is a time to embrace the amazing things your body can do, and to fuel it accordingly. Remember, you're growing another human and that's an incredible thing.

2. Tend to your cravings

Pregnancy can make you eat differently than you normally would. Our pregnancies had us stockpiling bagels and vegan cream cheese.

Whatever the case is for you, give yourself unconditional permission to nourish yourself and your baby. Intuitive eating doesn't involve counting calories or grams of fat, or measuring portion sizes. It's about listening to what your body is telling you.

Contrary to popular belief, cravings during pregnancy don't usually mean that you're deficient in something. They also don't mean you have to sway from your usual diet if you don't want to. For example, see our article on pregnancy meat cravings.

3.   Respect your hunger and fullness cues

Be cognizant of what your brain and belly are telling you, and make it simple. When you're feeling hungry, eat something. When you're getting full, slow down, take few minutes, and decide if it's time to stop eating. Pregnancy can be a cycle of ravenous hunger and intense nausea, so be sure to take care of yourself.

Sometimes it can be helpful to have keep healthy snacks available and within easy reach. That being said, we'll be the first to admit that junk foods often become even more appealing during pregnancy, so don't feel guilty if that's how you're feeling. Feed your body, and let go of any guilt.

4.   Quit the comparison game

This can admittedly be really hard to do. Remember that every woman's body goes through a unique transformation during pregnancy. Some women start to show almost immediately, while others don't seem to pop until they're in their third trimester. Weight gain, both in numbers and how the body carries it, also differs significantly between women.

There's no one right way to look during pregnancy (or any other time in life), and no reason to compare your pregnancy body to anyone else's. You're beautiful and uniquely you!

5.   Keep moving

We're not talking about training for a race, though pregnancy is like a marathon! Physical movement causes your brain to release endorphins, hormones known for having a calming and pleasant effect. Movement, in any form, can be very therapeutic during pregnancy.

If you enjoy running and feel good continuing, that's great. If your runs turn into walks, that's great too. Rather than attributing physical activity to burning calories, focus on how it feels to move your body. Endorphins are a much better motivator than numbers on a scale.

WAYS TO GET STARTED WITH INTUITIVE EATING FOR KIDS

Do you have a child who only likes three foods and only eats three bites? If so, you're not alone.

When kids have strange eating habits, it can drive you crazy. The picky eater especially.

Naturally, as parents, we fret that they're not getting enough nutrition or fuel, or that somehow their brains aren't going to develop properly.

When I was a kid, I hated steak. It was dry and boring, and I would poke at it with my knife while I itched to go back outside to the swing set before dark. One evening, my sister finished her meal and had already dashed back outside to the jungle gym. Without a dog in the house to sneak the remainder of my dinner, I tried compromising with my parents.

"If I have three more bites, can I go back outside?"

"Five more bites," they'd say. Or, more often, they'd probably just say "Catherine, eat your dinner."

My parents likely wanted to ensure that their scrawny kid was getting enough food. And while I don't think it damaged me in the long-term, there's a growing recognition that intuitive eating habits can bolster a child's long-term relationship with food and body image.

Intuitive eating is a complicated topic, and it can take years to undo the bizarre and sometimes harmful messages we've received about food through life. But here are several ways to get started with intuitive eating for kids.

1. Don't bargain

Negotiating skills are great (hello, I'm a lawyer!) but the dinner table is not the place. The "three more bites, Mom?" negotiations undercut a child's ability to identify their natural hunger and fullness cues. They may start to look at food as a project or a burden, rather than a source of pleasure and nutrition.

2. Avoid rewards for eating

Dangling dessert or screen time as a reward for a clean plate can send the wrong message to children. If your child shovels the food down to reach the reward, they will again have trouble identifying their own hunger and fullness. As tempting as it is to heap on the praise when your kid eats her vegetables, if she expects a reward every time, they are less likely to enjoy those foods in the long run.

3. Avoid eating as a reward

This one is similar, but slightly different. When your child wins the baseball game or gets all A's in school, you say, "You deserve a treat – let's go get ice cream!" Or "you cleaned up your room every day this week, so you can have french fries with dinner tonight."

But then, what if they lose the game, get mixed grades, or don't clean up their room? When certain foods, especially sugary foods or fried foods that our culture demeans as BAD, are used as a positive reward, children receive mixed signals. It sends a message that certain foods are off-limits until you earn them, or that eating and drinking are rewards for good behavior. Both of these messages interfere with our attempts to raise children who are intrinsically motivated and less self-centered.

4. Respect "I'm all done."

As frustrating as it can be, if your child claims she's done after only a couple bites, resist the urge to say "Oh no you're not! You've barely eaten a thing!" At most, I will ask "do you want more rice before you leave the table?" and respect her answer if she says she's full. Kids truly will eat if they're hungry. And, more often than not, they will get enough nutrition from various meals and snacks throughout the day. Try to chill a bit more.

5. Focus on the brainpower and bodypower of food

I'm sure you've heard this before (possibly from me), but please please please don't call foods "good" or "bad," or call yourself or ANYONE "good" or "bad" for eating certain foods. Focus instead on the way that nutrient-rich foods will help them run, do sports, read, and learn math. Continue to offer a wide range of food – even if they reject it 15 times, try try again and let them discover delicious fruits and vegetables they love.

6. Offer a variety of foods

Even though I mentioned fruits and vegetables, try not to become too obsessed with getting your kids to like "healthy" foods. An interesting study from 2000 of young girls who were pressured to eat healthy actually ended up restricting food, eating emotionally, and eating with abandon. (Carper, Fisher, Birch.) Admittedly, I do offer a lot of so-called "healthy" foods because that's mainly what I like, but sometimes we switch it up, especially at family events and birthday parties, where we mostly let her eat what she wants, until she's full. This way, kids don't feel like certain foods are off-limits. It may create some cake-induced sugar highs, but that's the fun of life, right?

7. Use a flexible routine

Routines are good for kids because they offer predictability. We offer three meals and two snacks, pretty much at the same time of day every day. My daughter knows that snack follows nap, and so on. But allow a little bit of flexibility in that routine. It's okay if your child isn't hungry for snack, or wants two full-sized breakfasts. Respond to what their body is telling them. This will help your child become an intuitive eater.

8. Be present for your food

As much as possible, we try to sit together at the table when we eat. Of course, sometimes you need to have a snack at the playground or offer a quick meal in the car on the way to piano lessons. But both children AND us grownups can more fully appreciate our food in a device-free zone, with each other's company. There's even something about the mid-day sunlight that makes our weekend lunches more relaxing and peaceful.

9. Become aware of emotionally-charged eating

If you eat in response to emotions – fear, sadness, boredom, anxiety – I'm certainly not going to shame you. But start to recognize it. I realized recently that I was bingeing on chocolate chips each time my 3 year-old went down for nap or bedtime, because those were the most stress-inducing parts of the day. Chocolate would calm me. And that's ok. Sometimes we just have to get through the day.

Emotional eating can take a while to address (and please do see a professional if you feel it is out of control) but begin with simple awareness that it's happening, so that you can better regulate the underlying emotion. Now, after a difficult bedtime, I lie down on the floor and breathe for a few minutes to process what just happened, and then let it go.

10. Get real about your own food choices

If you embark on a fad diet, like Keto or the Whole 30, and feel you need to hide it from your children, ask yourself why. Would you want your daughter, niece, or granddaughter emulating your choices? If the answer is no, reconsider whether it's the right choice for you. The best choice for you and your children is a style of eating that will last long-term and serve you well.

HOW DOES INTUITIVE EATING RELATE TO FEMINIST PARENTING?

Consent. One of the tenets of feminist parenting is to respect the child's body, emotions, and individuality. In order to respect our child's body, we create an atmosphere where they feel safe and respected. We talk a lot about consent here, but consent does not only govern when and if we touch each other.

Kids must also exercise authority over what they put in their bodies and when. This isn't to say that that you need to let your child eat only Oreos for every meal. Parents must still provide a range of food choices at certain times of the day. But the rest is up to our kids.

Body Image. In addition, we must distill for children the daily messages about appearance that infiltrate our lives. At a young age, kids learn which appearances are praised and which are not. Soon after, they learn how restriction of food can change their bodies. It's up to us to role model positive body image, help them to decipher the media images they see, and provide them with a strong foundation of independent thinking and problem-solving to value their worth beyond looks

CHAPTER 11

MEAL PLANNING: HOW TO MEAL PLAN IN INTUITIVE EATING

A big part of Intuitive Eating is learning to make decisions about what to eat based on what sounds and feels good in the moment. It may seem like intuitive eating and meal planning conflict, but I actually think they go hand in hand. When meal planning is done in a way that allows for flexibility and takes pleasure into consideration, meal planning can be a powerful ally in making peace with food. Learn how to meal plan in intuitive eating!

A big part of Intuitive Eating is learning to make decisions about what to eat based on what sounds and feels good in the moment. It may seem like intuitive eating and meal planning conflict, but I actually think they go hand in hand. When meal planning is done in a way that allows for flexibility and takes pleasure into consideration, meal planning can be a powerful ally in making peace with food.

If you live in NYC with basically every cuisine and type of food within a ten-block radius and have unlimited funds to order out, then yes, you can make food decisions 100% based on what sounds good in the moment because you have access to all the foods. For the rest of us, we need some semblance of a plan to make sure we have a variety of tasty foods available when hunger hits. Without a plan to have access to food, you'll be stuck making decisions about what to eat when your blood sugar is already running low. When your blood sugar is low and your brain is in need of nourishment, it's really hard to make a rational decision about what to eat.

Where meal planning goes wrong is when it's too rigid. Spending your entire Sunday on pinterest picking out recipes, creating a calendar of weekly meals, shopping, then prepping is...a lot. And what happens when Wednesday comes and you just have zero desire to eat barbecue salmon tacos and really you're just craving Thai? Or when you get called into a late meeting and get home ravenously hungry, will you still want to prepare that vegetable lasagna from scratch?

MEAL PREPAREDNESS VS. MEAL PLANNING

I like to think of meal planning more like meal preparedness. Because being prepared is really the point of it. Meal preparedness allows for you to have structure and makes it easy to honor your hunger because food is always available. It allows for you to build pleasure into your meals when you think about what foods you enjoy, not what you think you should eat. It's helpful for ensuring variety. And if you're working through eating disorder recovery or making peace with food in the Intuitive Eating process, planning ahead ensures you're prepared to build food challenges into your week.

With Intuitive Eating, meal planning isn't based on what you think you should eat, but rather what you want to eat.

There's no calories or points or whatever involved in the planning process.

Clients often share that they've tried meal planning in the past but got overwhelmed and gave up because it was taking hours and hours out of their weekend. It's no wonder when you have a dozen different diet rules you're trying to accommodate for! With meal planning for intuitive eating, nutrition may be a part of your decisions, but it's gentle nutrition. For example, I almost always include a vegetable in each meal when meal planning. If in looking at my week, I notice it's a bit skimpy in whole grains, I might purchase a whole grain pizza crust for my planned pizza night. Or if I realize I've been eating a lot of meat and cheese as of late, I might swap chicken for tofu in the stir fry I'm making.

MY STRATEGY FOR MEAL PLANING IN INTUITIVE EATING

How I meal plan can vary a bit based on whether I'm testing recipes for the blog or a brand I'm working with - which I usually am. But if I'm not doing recipe development, here's what I do:

PICK 2-4 "RECIPE" MEALS

Depending on whether my husband or I are traveling or have dinner plans, I'll pick 2-4 meals that are based on a recipe. I try to aim for 1-2 brand new recipes, which helps get my creativity going and gets me that variety I crave. For the others, I pick simple recipes that I basically already know how to make, like an old recipe from the blog. For example, if I pick a recipe for a stir-fry, that's super easy because I'm really familiar with how to stir-fry, and usually just have to glance at the recipe a few times during cooking. Or, I might pick out a recipe I know by heart, and try to switch it up a bit using different spices or condiments - again, this helps keep my variety craving taste buds happy.

HAVE 3-4 PANTRY MEALS ON HAND

Pantry meals are meals you can throw together with shelf stable ingredients and/or leftovers. I like to have a few different options available for easy meals. One of my favorites is sauteed onions and frozen spinach tossed with whole grain pasta and canned tuna. I'll add black olives and sun-dried tomatoes to dress it up. This is a great place to use up leftovers and prevent food waste.

Then we have room to go out to eat once a twice a week. I find that this leaves a lot of flexibility, because I don't have so much food on hand that I have to eat before it goes bad - if I'm craving pizza, we can just go out and get pizza and not worry about the spring mix starting to wilt.

On top of that, I always have ingredients for at least a couple different breakfast options, one sweet and one savory. Oatmeal, eggs, frozen fruit, yogurt, bread, and granola are pantry staples at our house, so usually it's some combination of those. But if I'm getting bored with that, I might pick out a new recipe or a different breakfast food.

Plus, there's snacks. We always have bars, dried fruit, nuts, fruit, yogurt, and granola on hand, so I usually pick up a couple other savory snacks to go with that, or plan to snack on leftovers.

OTHER STRATEGIES FOR HOW TO MEAL PLAN IN INTUITIVE EATING

Other strategies might work better for you. Some people are ok with eating a lot of the same foods and enjoy routine, while others want to try lots of different foods. Some people are cooking for big families with lots of different taste preferences, while others are cooking for one or two.

Here's some other strategies I've heard that may be useful:

THEME NIGHTS

I've heard of a few families doing this and it's such a great idea! Each night of the week is a different theme (i.e. Taco Tuesday, Pasta Wednesday, Roasted Chicken Sunday), and it helps a lot as you're trying to come up with meal ideas. You can stick with the usual ground beef taco recipe, or easily switch things up by doing a different protein and/or adding in a few different toppings.

5-4-3-2-1 PLAN

This is my friend Kylie's plan for grocery shopping when you don't have a plan, and I often pull it out when I don't feel like meal planning. The only change I make is that I get 5 vegetables and 3 carbs, since we already have a ton of grains and pasta in the pantry.

ORGANIZED MEAL PREP

Some people really do well by planning out each days meals and prepping on the weekend. While it feels like a lot for me, others like that structure. My friend Lindsey has some really great resources for making meal planning/prep more streamlined and simplified.

OUTSOURCE

If you can afford it, outsource! Get a meal delivery service, like Blue Apron or Hello Fresh. I also really like Fresh 20, which provides weekly meal plans for 5 budget friendly meals using 20 different ingredients that are really simple to make. The downside to this with Intuitive Eating is that you don't get to pick meals based on what sounds good to you, but I think there's enough flexibility in there to where you can go out to eat or pick something up to make if you're craving something different.

At the end of the day, whatever you decide to do for meal planning, it needs to have some flexibility built in. Think of it as flexible structure.

MORE TIPS FOR HOW TO MEAL PLAN IN INTUITIVE EATING

COOK ONCE, EAT TWICE

Plan for leftovers! I like to use mine for lunch, or you can always cook extra of one item, and plan to use it for leftovers later in the week. For example, I made a pizza topped with sauteed fennel, corn and tomatoes earlier in the week, and later, I used the extra sauteed vegetables to round out a pasta meal kit (this one by Modern Table Meals - thanks for the samples!)

FREEZE EXTRAS

It makes sense if you're making something like soup or chili to prepare extra, but you probably don't want to eat chili for a week. Just freeze the extras, which are great a month later when you don't feel like cooking!

PURCHASE FOOD THAT LASTS LONGER

You'll have more flexibility if you don't feel like you have to eat the food your purchased before it goes bad. Get sturdier vegetables, like cauliflower, zucchini, or carrots, or even shop frozen/canned.

GET GROCERY DELIVERIES

The most annoying part of meal planning is forgetting something, which I inevitably do at least once a week. Usually I bug my husband to stop by the store on the way home from work, but also, grocery delivery, like Shipt (client) is a huge time-saver.

THINK ABOUT HOW MUCH TIME YOU HAVE TO COOK

Like, if you know you're working long hours one week, don't plan out lasagna from scratch. Go get yourself some Stouffers.

THINK ABOUT WHAT INGREDIENTS YOU ALREADY HAVE ON HAND

Reduce food waste by looking at what ingredients you already have on hand!

CHAPTER 12

INTUITIVE EATING TIPS AND RECIPES

1. Aim for Satisfaction

One of the key intuitive eating principles is aiming for satisfaction. "Aiming for satisfaction is the beauty of food and really enjoying food," says Melanie. If you're like us, you probably feel happy and satisfied when you're full. So Melanie showed us a satiating twist on the popular avocado toast.

- **AVOCADO CRACKERS**

Ingredients:

- 2 ripe avocados, sliced

- 2 medium heirloom tomatoes, rough chopped

- 1 pepper, such as corno di toro peppers, rough chopped

- 1 purple bunching or green onion, minced

- 1-2 tsp. fresh lime juice

- Pinch sea salt

- Garnish: apricot, bronze fennel, and edible flowers (such as bachelor button petals)

Directions:

- Chop all ingredients.

- Gently toss ingredients with a fork.

- Spoon avocado mixture on to raw dehydrated crackers.

- Enjoy with edible flowers, bronze fennel, and apricots or peaches

2. Respect Your Body

Next on our list of intuitive eating principles – appreciate our bodies! "You gotta respect your body; this is your home," insists Evelyn. "The longest relationship you'll have for life is your body." So be good to your body and fill it with good things – like Melanie's lunchtime spring sage and mint salad.

- **SPRING LETTUCE SALAD**

Ingredients (Mint & Pineapple Sage Dressing):

- ¼ cup lemon juice

- ½ cup organic extra virgin olive oil

- Pinch sea salt

- 3-4 stems fresh herbs, such as Moroccan Mint and Pineapple Sage, rough chopped.

Directions (Mint & Pineapple Sage Dressing):

- Squeeze lemon juice into a jar.

- Add twice as much olive oil as lemon juice to the jar.

- Shake. Taste. Add more oil if too lemony. Add more lemon if too oily.

- Add pinch sea salt and fresh herbs; Moroccan mint and pineapple sage.

- Shake. Save to toss with salad.

Salad Ingredients:

- 2 cups of different varieties of lettuce, such as glacier lettuce (ice lettuce) and cimmaron (wild red lettuce), torn

- ½ Armenian cucumber, sliced

- 1 red beet, formanova, thinly sliced

- ¼ cup walnuts

- Garnish: red veined sorrel, edible flowers: violas

Salad Directions:

- Pour a few teaspoons of dressing onto the beets. Toss. Let rest for 5-10 minutes.

- Place lettuce and cucumbers into medium bowl.

- Pour the remainder of the dressing over the lettuce and cucumbers.

- Lightly toss to coat all lettuce leaves and cucumbers with the dressing.

- Plate salad with layers of the lettuce, beets, and walnuts.

- Garnish with red veined sorrel and violas.

3. Reject Diet Cult

Finally, to eat intuitively is to say goodbye to formal diets. "Reject diet culture. Nobody can be the boss of you, only you can," Evelyn urges. No one can tell you what or how much of something is right for your body. So Melanie's final recipe says no to diets and yes to zucchini pasta for dinner.

- **ZUCCHINI PASTA & RAW TOMATO SAUCE**

Ingredients:

- 1 large zucchini, spiralized

- Amethyst basil and purple pansies for garnish

Tomato Sauce Ingredients:

- *3*-4 red heirloom tomatoes, rough chopped

- 1 pepper (corno di toro), rough chopped

- ¼ cup sun-dried tomatoes, soaked in water for 1 hour, then drained.

- 2 purple bunching onions, minced

- 3-5 stems, oregano, torn

- 3-5 stems, green (Genovese) basil, torn

- Pinch sea salt

- 2 tbsp olive oil

Tomato Sauce Directions:

- Process all ingredients in food processor, keeping the sauce chunky. After blended, taste and adjust to suit your taste.

Cashew Cream Sauce Ingredients:

- 1.5 cups raw cashews, soaked 2-4 hours in water, drain.

- 2 tbsp fresh lemon juice

- ½ tsp lemon zest

- 2 tbsp nutritional yeast

- 2 tbsp water

- Pinch sea salt

- 2 or more tbsp. water, as needed for creaminess.

- Additional lemon, nutritional yeast, and salt for taste.

Cashew Cream Sauce Directions:

- Blend all ingredients in food processor, until smooth.

- Taste. Add additional lemon, nutritional yeast, or sea salt to suit your taste.

Plating:

- Toss spiralized zucchini with three-fourths of the tomato sauce.

- Place zucchini with sauce into bowl.

- Top with the remaining tomato sauce and cashew cream sauce.

- Garnish with amethyst basil and purple pansies.

Is your mouth watering yet? Now you've got three intuitive eating principles and recipes to help you eat your way to happiness.

- INTUITIVE EATING: SUGAR-FREE CROCKPOT APPLESAUCE

Ingredients:

- 8 organic apples for 2 pints of applesauce, including some tasters for you too

- 1 organic lemon

- organic cinnamon

- Crockpot (This is the exact crockpot I have!)

- 1/4 c of filtered, alkaline water

Directions:

Step one: Slice your apples into thin strips. I take the super easy approach here, but feel free to make it as intensive as you like. I simply wash my apples and chop them up, one side at a time until all that is left is the core. I do not peel my apples, but if you wish to do so, here's a peeler/corer I've never used and an apple corer, which I've also never used. (I'll always tell you if for any reason I haven't used something! :)). I wanted you to have some options. OK, now that we got that out of the way…

Step two: Place apple slices in crockpot. Slice the lemon in half and squeeze the juice of the lemon over the apple slices. Add the water as well.

Step three: Cinnamon it up! I do this by eye, but you can do 1-2T of cinnamon per 8-apple batch. I have over cinnamoned (now a word) and that isn't so good. But I now focus on giving the apples a healthy dusting of cinnamon on the top layer of apples visible in the crockpot.

Step four: Cook on high for 3 hours or low for 6 hours. Come by and stir the apples occasionally to help support the juices and cinnamon in mixing in well. You can overcook this – know because I've done it. So don't do anything more than a half hour over on either of these. I'll often turn it to low after 3 hours on high and do 30 minutes on low if I want it to be a little more cooked down. But more than that and it's not so great. Also, feel free to bless the applesauce while it's cooking.

Step five: If you don't eat it all right then and there, put into 2 pint jars or smaller jars if you like. This is amazing solo or with grain-free granola and seeds (and with pancakes!) or as a side dish to anything or with a spoonful of Coconut Bliss Infinite Coconut (if you're into that kind of thing – organic agave appears in the Bliss, so I allow for this on special occasions and usually on the weekends or when I won't be having client sessions). Enjoy! Xo

- **GRAIN-FREE EGG SANDWICH DELIGHT**

Ingredients:

- 1-2 organic eggs (1 egg for every sandwich you're making, so adjust accordingly)

- 1T of Primal Kitchen organic avocado mayo*

- 1/2 c of sautéed organic kale or spinach*

- Organic garlic salt, to taste

- 1/2 an organic avocado, sliced

- Simple Mills Grain-free bread, prepared ahead of time

- Organic coconut oil, for coating fry pan

- Organic avocado oil, as needed for sautéing the kale and/or spinach

Preparation:

Step one: The toast, starting as bread. Bake this the day before you make this recipe OR when you have an hour at minimum before you need to eat. My friends (well, they don't know we're friends yet) over at Simple Mills have done it again with their Artisan Bread mix. I bake mine into a loaf. You can also add 1T of organic garlic salt and 3T of organic rosemary to make this bread even more savory. I use organic avocado oil as my preferred oil for the mix as well.

Step two: Coat sauté pan with organic avocado oil and place chopped organic kale/spinach in the pan. Lightly salt with organic garlic salt. Cover and move to step three…

Step three: Coat a small frying pan with organic coconut oil. Fry up your egg(s). I recommend placing the cracked egg in a medium-high heat pan, salting with organic sea salt and then covering the pan and reducing the temp to low for up 1-3 minutes. When it's ready, flip and cover again for 1-3 minutes – depending on the strength of your stove.

Step four: Toast the grain-free bread if it's not already warm. Spread the avo mayo on the toast, followed by some of the sautéed kale/spinach, topped by the fried egg. Then top with slices of the organic avocado.

Step five: Get a hearty cloth napkin if you plan to eat this with your hands. Or if you're really classy (please note, I ate this with my hands, alone ;)) get a knife and fork and eat it like a real lady/gentleman

- **HEALTHY BREAKFAST: GRAIN-FREE BANANA GRANOLA PANCAKES**

Ingredients:

- 1 box of Simple Mills Pancake mix (to make: 1.5 c of the mix, 3 organic eggs, 3T unsweetened vanilla hemp milk, 2T organic coconut oil)

- 1 1/2 large organic banana, sliced

- 1 cup of Backroads Coconut Crunch grain-free granola

- 1 T of each of your seeds for seed cycling. I was on flax seeds and pumpkin seeds for this recipe.

- 2T of organic maple syrup

- 5T of organic coconut oil

Preparation:

Step one: Make up pancake mix, using all that is outlined in the first bullet point. Add the sliced banana to the mix. Optional: You may wish to add the granola at this point too or wait like I did – use your intuition for what is best. Use coconut oil to coat a medium-sized sauté pan or griddle. Begin making your pancakes!

Step two: Once the pancakes are just about complete, place the maple syrup and coconut oil in a small saucepan on low heat. Stir together and cover. Heat until warmed and continue to stir until well mixed. Optional: You may replace coconut oil with organic grass-fed butter – your choice. Taste to see if you need to add more butter/oil so that it is not too sweet. Once you have the sweet level you desire, move on to step three...

Step three: Stack 3 pancakes on a plate. Pour as much of the yummy syrup blend as you are called to. Optional: You may choose to use organic Coconut Nectar instead of our maple blend – your choice.

Step four: Pour 1/4 cup of the granola over the pancakes and syrup. Pour the 2T of seeds for your seed cycling over next.

Step five: Bless these pancakes and enjoy!

- **COFFEE REPLACEMENT: ORGANIC DANDELION ROOT TEA LATTE WITH SUPERFOOD CREAMER**

Ingredients:

- 1 teabag of organic roasted dandelion root tea
- 12-16oz, boiling hot filtered water
- 2T of Laird's Superfood Creamer, original vegan

Preparation:

Step one: Pour hot water into your fave mug (not pictured here as I wanted you to see the creamy deliciousness through the glass mug!).

Step two: Place teabag in water and leave in for 1 minute before adding creamer.

Step three: Add creamer and stir.

Step four: Bless this drink and enjoy!

CHAPTER 13

WHAT IS BODY RESPECT?

If you struggle with the idea of loving your body and find that it feels like a foreign and unattainable concept, we get it. The true goal is that you start to move from a place of body hatred to a place of body respect so that you can take care of your body both physically and mentally. Read on for more about the difference between body love and body respect, plus steps you can take to respect and take care of your body.

The language around bodies and health can be confusing and oftentimes misleading. When Alissa and I begin work with clients to heal their body image, we often hear: "It seems like I'm just supposed to wake up one day and suddenly love everything about my body – that's never going to happen!" We're grateful for such awesome clients who open up and share these thoughts with us because – yes, it is unrealistic!

Diet culture messages imply – or directly say – that to be healthy, to be happy and to be successful you must be thin. And while hashtags like #bodylove and #bodypositive started as a way to promote positive body image messages, at this point it often feels like these hashtags have been taken over by thin women with socially acceptable body types.

This can make the idea of loving your body even more daunting.

Which is why we like to shift from thinking about loving your body to instead working on moving towards feeling neutral about your body and respecting your body. Can you move from body dissatisfaction to body neutrality? Can you spend less time thinking about and worrying about your body, even if you don't love it looks? And can you respect your body no matter how you feel about it?

Body Love vs. Body Respect

Newsflash: you don't have to love everything about your body and, in fact, it's unrealistic to think we will love every single thing about our bodies. This is where body respect comes in: it is really difficult to take good care of something that you don't respect. So rather than a goal of loving your body, aiming for body respect is more realistic and ultimately more important when it comes to taking care of yourself.

Even on the days when you may not feel your body 'looks' up to your standards, it's still doing so many things to keep you alive and participating in your life. Think about all the amazing things our bodies do for us: it allows us to hug our loved ones, birth babies, participate in social activities, convert food into energy, and even just get out of bed in the morning.

These are all things that, regardless of how you feel about your body image today, your body is still doing for you or helping you do. So what does body respect look like? Here are some examples:

- Honoring your hunger signals, eating something each and every time your body tells you that it's hungry.

- Dressing in clothes that fit and feel comfortable.

- Talking to yourself with compassion and kindness

- Moving your body in a way that feels good to you

Bodies are meant to look and be different. And regardless of what they look like on the outside, they're doing a lot for you on the inside. Try to take some time to think about the following questions:

- How would you respect your body more if it looked differently?

- How does waiting until you look a certain way to give yourself respect align with your values?

- What would it be like to take care of your body and show it respect now, instead of waiting until you reach a certain goal?

- What would it be like to eat and move in a way that felt good instead of in the hopes of changing your body?

- What would it feel like to spend less time preoccupied with how your body looks or you wished it looked?

WAYS TO PRACTICE BODY RESPECT

1. Diversify your social media feed

We say this all the time over here, but diversifying the images you see and the messages you get about bodies, health, food, and beauty is a huge step towards feeling better in your body. Here are some of favorite Instagram accounts that feature a variety of diverse body sizes, shapes, ages, genders, abilities and colors.

2. Buy comfortable clothes

If your clothes (this includes underwear and bras) are tight or don't fit well, it will be a constant daily reminder. Don't wait until you are at a certain size to buy new clothes – dress the body that you have now. Treat your body with respect by buying yourself clothes that fit you, clothes that you like, and clothes that you feel comfortable in.

3. Practice self-care

Do nice things for your body. Think about ways that you can take care of your body, both physically and mentally. This could be meditation, deep breathing, movement, running a bubble bath, watching a favorite tv show, taking a walk with a friend, using some luxurious body lotion, or reading a good book. Check out this blog post on Building a Self-Care Toolbox for more ideas.

4. Stop body checking and comparing yourself to others

Remind yourself that you don't know anyone else's story. They may have the "perfect" body, but you don't know what's going on inside of them. We all look different and bodies come in all shapes and sizes. Body diversity exists naturally and it is a beautiful thing. Try to catch yourself when you find yourself comparing yourself to others and put the focus back on yourself.

5. Don't tear apart your body

When you're feeling down about yourself or your body, work on not spiraling into a negative script of things you're unhappy with or wish to change. Instead, think about how you'd talk to and support a friend who was feeling the same way. What would you say to them? It's likely that you'd show them much more compassion than you do yourself. Try to then show that same compassion to yourself and stop the negative self-talk in its tracks.

6. Focus on what your body does for you

What are some compliments you can give yourself that have nothing to do with what you look like? Make a list of at least 15 things that you like about yourself. If this is difficult, think about the things you love and appreciate about your friends and loved ones. When you do give compliments to others, try to do so in a way that has nothing to do with their looks or their body. Some ideas: "Your smile lights up the room!"; "You're a great listener"; "Thank you for always showing up and making me feel heard"; "You are so fun to be around"; or "I love the way you think.

CONCLUSION

If you think you could benefit from learning more about intuitive eating, there are ways to get started.

Without judgment, start taking stock of your own eating behaviors and attitudes. When you eat, ask yourself if you're experiencing physical or emotional hunger.

If it's physical hunger, try to rank your hunger/fullness level on a scale of 1–10, from very hungry to stuffed. Aim to eat when you're hungry but not starving. Stop when you're comfortably full — not stuffed.

With intuitive eating, how you eat is just as important as what you eat.

Letting your own internal cues of hunger and fullness guide your eating can lead to improved body image and quality of life